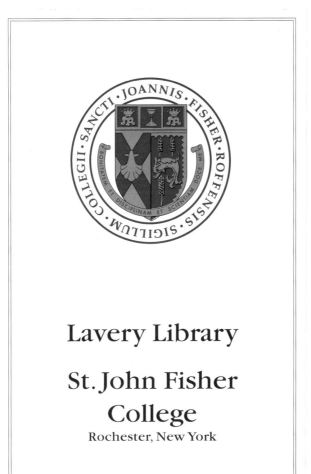

making good

making good

**How Young People Cope with
Moral Dilemmas at Work**

WENDY FISCHMAN

BECCA SOLOMON

DEBORAH GREENSPAN

HOWARD GARDNER

harvard university press

CAMBRIDGE, MASSACHUSETTS

LONDON, ENGLAND

2004

PRINTED IN THE UNITED STATES OF AMERICA

Library of Congress Cataloging-in-Publication Data
Making good : how young people cope with moral dilemmas at work /
Wendy Fischman . . . [et al.].
p. cm.
Includes bibliographical references and index.
ISBN 0-674-01194-5 (alk. paper)
1. Work—Moral and ethical aspects. 2. Professional employees. I. Fischman, Wendy.

HD4905.M344 2004
174—dc22   2003058738

To Julie J. Kidd
and
To Louise and Claude Rosenberg
In admiration and with gratitude

Preface

I T IS OFTEN SAID THAT the quality of social scientists' research is proportional to the distance they maintain from the objects of their investigation. Yet it is also clear that many social scientists study issues that are of deep personal concern. It is surely no coincidence that psychoanalyst Erik Erikson, confused about his own family background, identified the identity crisis; or that, some years before the decision on *Brown vs. Board of Education* was handed down, the pioneering black psychologists Kenneth Clark and Mamie Clark investigated the preferences for white dolls among young Negro children. "Research is me-search," goes the frequently heard quip.

Our interest in the ethical dispositions of young workers arose from our studies of adult professionals and from our casual observations of trends in U.S. society. But in ways that we could not have anticipated, we were drawn into the very issues that we had been investigating "from afar."

To begin with, there was the nature of our research team. While we worked together for years in a collegial atmosphere, it was obvious that we were three young persons (all recently graduated from college) and one older person (who celebrated his sixtieth birthday as this book was being edited). The issues of training, mentoring, role models, work pressures, temptations to cut corners were not just abstract social scientific concepts—they were the stuff of our daily work lives. As three female researchers and one male principal investigator, we continually negotiated our roles and responsibilities: securing funding, interviewing, analyzing, writing. Once one looks beyond wrinkles on the skin, it is far less clear who is the mentor and who are the mentees. The marks of each and every one of us can be found throughout the manuscript.

We were also drawn into these issues beyond the confines of our offices. As we were completing the manuscript in the spring of 2003, the media were reporting on the case of Jayson Blair, a highly touted young reporter for the *New York Times*. Blair had not only made numerous errors in his reporting; he had also invented details, faked receipts, lied about his whereabouts, and plagiarized from at least one other newspaper. Yet despite this woefully unprofessional performance, he had been promoted and rewarded again and again by his superiors. And this had happened not at a small newspaper, but at one of the most respected papers in the world, one that we ourselves cited as a locus of good work.

Before the story broke, Jayson Blair, a beginning reporter at the *New York Times*, had been nominated to participate in our study. Perhaps characteristically, he did not show up for the interview, said that he would come later, and never did. He was not alone; young journalists proved to be the least reliable of our subjects. But his case brought out many other stories of young workers-in-training and young professionals whose work was careless, compromised, or simply bad. Our collection of clippings about students who cheated in school or misrepresented their achievements, job applicants who distorted their record for future employers, young accountants who contributed to fraud at major accounting companies, thickened with every passing week. Suddenly the topic of our study was front-page news. The *New*

York Times decided to cover our study because of its timeliness, but ultimately did not include the connection to their own discredited Jayson Blair.

Whatever the lore about social science, we are no longer innocent. We realize that the issues about which we write—a sense of mission, a question of role models, and the capacity to take and pass the mirror test—are not just about others, but also about ourselves. Readers can see for themselves, in the Blair case, in the daily news, and in their own experience, how relevant our findings are. As we discovered in pursuing our research, these issues concern not just young professionals; they concern everyone.

In the course of our study we incurred a great many debts, both professional and personal. Elizabeth Knoll, our senior editor at Harvard University Press, is a master of the difficult art of combining encouragement with tough-minded criticism, and the book has benefited from both. Also at HUP we thank Maria Ascher (whose skill and patience were invaluable), Sheila Barrett, Kirsten Giebutowski, Mary Ann Lane, and Rose Ann Miller. At the GoodWork Project, special thanks to Kim Barberich, Lynn Barendsen, Michelle Cheuk, Greg Feldman, Grace Lam, Marcy LeLacheur, Paula Marshall, Mimi Michaelson, Ryan Modri, Jenna Moskowitz, Jeanne Nakumara, Kim Powell, Heather Rebmann, Jen Reese, and Jeff Solomon. For their help in furthering our understanding of the three domains, we thank Betty Ann Browser, Bob Colby, Mike Cummings, Ron Jenkins, Robert Kuttner, Jonathan Levy, and most especially the participants of our study, who took the time to share their perspectives and stories. Thanks, as well, to Steve Seidel, Barbara Schneider, and James Youniss. In addition to this professional help, we also acknowledge our families. Even as we were writing about issues of balance, we ourselves were not immune to the pushes and pulls of married life, children, and graduate schools. The support that our families provided was essential for our work.

It is always difficult to raise money for social science research; after all, it neither directly saves thousands of lives nor enables one to kill tens of thousands of people. But raising money is especially hard in uncertain economic times, when foundations have no mailbox labeled "Professional Ethics," "Workers in Training," or "Good Work." For our overall study of GoodWork, we are immensely fortunate to have received funding from the Bauman Foundation, the Berger-Mittlemann Family Trust, the Carnegie Corporation of New York, the Nathan Cummings Foundation, the J. Epstein Foundation, the Fetzer Institute, the Ford Foundation, the William and Flora Hewlett Foundation, Thomas E. Lee, the Pew Charitable Trusts, the Jesse Phillips Foundation Fund, the Ross Family Charitable Foundation, the Spencer Foundation, the Thrive Foundation, and the John Templeton Foundation.

For our study of young workers and young professionals, we are indebted to three generous funders who are also three admirable human beings: Louise Rosenberg and Claude Rosenberg, whose Family Foundation supported the "Origins of Good Work" study, and Julie J. Kidd, president of the Christian Johnson Endeavor Foundation, who supported our "Young Professionals" study. We approached these remarkable philanthropists in the mid-1990s, when our GoodWork project was merely a gleam in our eye, and asked them if they would underwrite such investigations. Not only did they immediately agree to do so; but when we needed additional funds to complete our research, they again came to our aid. It has been a pleasure and an honor to have the support of these people, whose own work demonstrates the highest standards of ethics and excellence. We thank them in one of the few ways available to scholars: by dedicating this book to them.

Contents

making good

1

Making the Good Worker

IT WOULD BE COMFORTING to think that the acts of corporate malfeasance which have come to light in the United States at the start of the twenty-first century are isolated events, and that the world of work is generally in fine shape. It would also be naïve. There is a distressing amount of unacceptable behavior across professions and in a variety of workplaces. With numbing regularity, the media tell of scholars who misrepresent their credentials; journalists who blur the line between fact and invention; politicians who accept bribes or are beholden to well-heeled contributors; ministers, priests, and rabbis who abuse their positions of trust; lawyers who condone perjury on the part of their clients; and physicians who value personal gain more than the welfare of their patients.

Whether the situation in various professions is worse today than in earlier times, or simply disappointing in comparison to the public's expectations, is difficult to gauge. Reflecting on the scandals at Enron, Arthur Andersen, WorldCom, and other American corporations, Federal Reserve Board chairman Alan Greenspan commented, "It is not that humans have become any more greedy than in generations past. It is that the avenues to express greed had grown so enormously."[1] Yet there is no question that many accomplished professionals who should know better are betraying their calling, and neither their fellow professionals nor members of the general public seem able to reverse these disturbing trends.

But where do such flawed workers come from? Where do they get their ethical sense, or their lack thereof? If one had observed these professionals in the course of their education, or on their first or second jobs, what would they have been like? Are they formerly ethical workers who have lost their sense of direction, or individuals who never understood the core values of their profession in the first place, or persons who seek to do the right thing but find themselves overwhelmed by circumstances? And—a question of special importance for society (and for this book)—how might it be possible to educate a greater proportion of admirable workers, ones who have a strong ethical compass, know the right thing to do, and proceed to do it even when it apparently conflicts with their immediate self-interest? What can we all learn from young people who seem to be on track toward a life of good work?

Three Dilemmas at the Workplace

In 1996 the GoodWork Project began studying dozens of young workers as they encountered situations that tested their professional mettle.[2] The experiences of three of those young workers were particularly instructive.

An aspiring journalist we'll call Bill (the names of all the participants have been changed), a male in his early twenties, was an undergraduate at Harvard University and associate managing editor of the *Harvard Crimson*. To gain work experience, Bill had interned during the summer at the *Journal News* in suburban New York and at MSNBC, the online version of NBC News. During his internship, Bill had often felt that his concept of good journalism conflicted with the editors' notions of effective practice. He was frequently urged to pursue sensational stories and to report them in ways that he considered irresponsible. One day he was asked to cover the funeral of a sixteen-year-old baseball star in a local community. Arriving at the funeral, he found it packed with friends and family who were sharing fond memories of the boy. Bill came back to the newsroom "hoping to write a very poetic piece." Upon his return, however, he learned that a sensational news-event had occurred: John F. Kennedy, Jr., had disappeared while piloting a small plane. As he recalled later, his editors insisted: "You have to write the other story, the funeral thing, in an hour, because you've got to go to the mall to interview people about what they think about this missing celebrity." Bill was torn between his journalistic values and those of his editors. He felt a responsibility to report on the young athlete's funeral because it "meant so very much to the small community of people" to whom he was reporting. Instead, he was ordered to cover an event that he considered "just the next opportunity for the media to haul out the funeral theme music for their promos and the fancy graphics." It seemed to him like "a dirty moment for journalism" and confirmed for him "what is wrong about the media today."

David was a twenty-seven-year-old postdoctoral fellow in evolutionary genetics at Stanford University. He had written a paper advancing new ideas on the evolution of sex determination, and presented it at a few professional conferences before submitting it for publication. He was enthusiastic and passionate about helping others in his field. At one conference, he discussed his work with Peter, a graduate student in a different lab. According to David, Peter was delighted to hear the presentation, since he had faced a similar obstacle in his own work and had not yet come up with a solution. Pleased by the opportunity to share his ideas with a peer, David acceded to Peter's request for more detailed information: "Great, I'll send you materials if you want." David followed through on this promise but never heard back from Peter. Some months later, David was scanning Peter's webpage and found his own method presented as if it had been devised by Peter. He was completely taken aback. "I thought that I was in a field where I was a little bit removed from the competitive aspect and the cut-throat behavior. So this was an unwelcome reminder that you're never immune from that kind of thing." The episode proved a pivotal moment in David's early career. Not only did it shake his trust in his peers, but it also taught him that sharing information with others might deprive him of recognition for years of original research.

Martha, a thirty-year-old African American professional actor, was sent a play by her friend Tom. At first she was excited about being involved in the production, because the script was based on the oral histories of American slaves. Tom was white, however, and as the ensemble began preparing the show "a lot of people from all over the country, black, authorities on theater, on literature . . . big, famous people . . . came to fight and protest the play." The main complaint of the protesters seemed to be that a white man was presenting African American voices and stories. Martha was filled with conflicting emotions. She felt allegiance to the African American community but she also believed in the social and artistic value of her friend's play. She sought to mediate among feelings of responsibility to her race, her art, and her friend: "I felt almost torn because here I am—I am a black woman—and it's a play about something that's very sensitive to me, and automatically I want to just jump to the other side without having anything to do with him [Tom]. But knowing him and being his friend made me say, 'Okay, look at the whole picture here.'"

Three young professionals, drawn from three different realms, each wrestling with the kinds of conflicts that arise regularly in the workplace. Bill, a young journalist, was struggling with authority: his editors wanted one thing, but his own sense of journalism called for another course of behavior. David, a young geneticist, was caught in an imbroglio with a peer. His inclination was to share his methodological discoveries but he was brought up short by the risk that his ideas could be used without any acknowledgment. Martha, a young actor, was experiencing an inner conflict: she was searching for a stance toward her friend's play that would satisfy her own values.

Stepping away from these conflicts, we as researchers posed the broad question that this book seeks to answer: How, at a time of rapid change, when market forces are extraordinarily powerful, do young people of talent and passion cope with the ethical conflicts that inevitably arise in the workplace? Or, to use the terminology of our study: How is it possible for young people to carry out "good work"?

"Good Work" in a Healthy Society

Some facets of life are so important and so pervasive that they risk being taken for granted. Nearly all adults spend the majority of their waking lives at work. Needless to say, it is highly desirable that they like and are productive on their jobs—otherwise the decades leading up to retirement will be depressing at best. The rest of society has an equally large stake in the individual's work life. Society has the right to ask that each person carry out work which is "good" in both senses of the word: whether philosophers or plumbers, sociologists or service workers, people should perform their work with skill (make it technically good) *and* should do so in a way that responds to the needs of society at large (make it morally good).

This view of the "adult world of work" has clear resonance for young people. At some point between early childhood and adulthood, individuals must make two consequential decisions. One entails selecting the line of work to be pursued; if the person chooses to enter a profession, the decision may be made relatively early and may involve many years of formal training. The second decision pertains to the kind of worker that the individual will become. In particular, will he or she prove to be someone who behaves in a responsible and ethical manner? Or someone who scorns such an ideal, cutting every possible corner and perhaps even committing acts that are illegal? Or someone with admirable intentions who folds under pressure?

On occasion, one or both of these decisions may be made with lightning speed, reminiscent of Saul's conversion on the road to Damascus; far more commonly, however, they are worked out painstakingly, over a good many years. In industrialized countries, most young people consider a variety of careers, and some individuals may move into a new line of work as late as the fourth decade of their lives. As for the practices that a worker exhibits from day to day, rarely are these fixed in early life. Unless one harbors a theological conviction that people are born "good" or "evil" (either individually or collectively), one's own moral compass is constructed gradually over many years, based on myriad experiences and myriad personal and communal reactions to these experiences. Even in cases where an individual's personal moral identity as saint or sinner has apparently been consolidated at a relatively early age, the processes by which the person fashions his or her behavior "on the job" are constantly being created and revised.

In what follows, we are concerned with the making of workers—more specifically, with the way in which developing human beings become, or fail to become, good workers. We will ask what it means to become an expert—what it means to be good at one's job. But we will focus more closely on the second connotation of "good"—on what it means to become a professional who behaves in an ethical or responsible manner. Though this second sense of "good" may impose an extra burden on the nascent worker, we believe that this additional requirement is ultimately energizing. Moreover, because a healthy society depends crucially on individuals who will be "good workers" in a dual sense, all members of society have a high stake in the nurturance of good work across the professional landscape.

The Path to This Study

Three broad lines of scholarly research are relevant to our investigation. The first explores the steps by which a person becomes an expert in a domain. Many studies confirm that it takes thousands of hours of practice—over perhaps a decade—for a novice to become an expert.[3] Sometimes the potential expert emerges early in life; the "prodigy" is a young person who precociously achieves an adult level of expertise in a given domain, such as playing chess or performing on the violin.[4] More commonly, young people exhibit a range of interests and abilities and only gradually come to focus on their ultimate area of achievement.[5] The latter is the typical pattern for most professions; it is the rare ten-year-old whose heart is set on becoming a lawyer, an accountant, or a university professor.

While we as researchers were personally interested in the origins of talent, this study was not framed to secure data relevant to debates about the relative contributions of nature versus nurture. It assumes that family support, good teaching, and intrinsic and extrinsic motivation play an essential role in the development of young professionals.[6] What is important here is the recognition that, at least in some cases, individuals display early and long-lasting fascination with a societal activity, and that such fascination may well translate into a career decision.

Like the development of expertise, the moral development of young people has been much researched. The pioneering works of Jean Piaget and Lawrence Kohlberg have shown that young people pass through a series of developmental stages of moral reasoning.[7] Young schoolchildren are oriented toward power and the egocentric fulfillment of their own wishes: "That's mine—don't you dare take it from me." Pre-adolescents adhere to rules and conventions, and assume a strict "equality" orientation toward questions of justice: "Let's make sure everyone gets exactly the same-size helping." Adolescents often assume a highly relativistic view of morality: "Who am I to judge others?" Sophisticated moral reasoners take into account motivations and intentions; recognize that individuals (for example, those from historically mistreated groups) may have privileged claims on justice; and hold—in the spirit of Mahatma Gandhi or Martin Luther King, Jr.— that sometimes it is proper to break the law for moral reasons, provided that one is willing to accept the consequences of such illegal actions.

When it comes to the relation between moral judgment and moral action, however, there is little consensus.[8] While some authorities posit a close fit between these two spheres, others stress that moral behavior in a particular context follows its own, possibly idiosyncratic course. Unfortunately, instead of focusing on actual moral judgments individuals have made, most of the studies rely on individuals' judgments of hypothesized dilemmas in interviews, under controlled laboratory conditions, or, less frequently, in school settings.

A third line of study probes the development of individuals' knowledge and interest about the world of work. During early and middle childhood, most people assume that they can pursue any career that catches their fancy; they focus heavily on external characteristics (the kind of uniform that is worn, the physical locale, the hours of work each day), and change their professional aspirations whenever they see fit.[9] By the time they reach adolescence, they begin to differ in their orientation toward work. Less sophisticated individuals continue to imagine that they can assume all possible roles ("Of course I can be a pro basketball player, a neurosurgeon, or president"), failing to realize that luck and hard work both play a role in determining career paths and ultimate success.[10] Such persons can benefit from realistic career counseling and career exploration.[11] To help discover their own potential, some young people also take interest inventories or personality protocols, such as the Strong Interest Inventory (SII) and the Campbell Interest and Skill Survey (CISS).[12] More sophisticated or committed adolescents have already embarked on a clear career path—for example, by studying hard so that they can gain admission to a selective college, or by pursuing extracurricular activities that relate to an adult role, or by arranging mentorships or summer jobs that introduce them to possible professions.[13] The young people surveyed in our study were drawn principally from this highly motivated group.

While developmental research on expertise, morality, and work continues to be pursued in instructive ways, there has been little effort to relate these strands of study to one another. For the most part, the literature on talent and expertise presupposes that the gifted child will eventually become a professional, but does not examine the transition from a "talent life" to a "work life."[14] For their part, analysts of moral development either consider the person as a unified moral thinker or actor, or they view moral thought and behavior as determined largely by situational factors—for example, opportunities for cheating in the classroom. Such investigations do not adequately confront the issue of how individuals might deal with ethical issues that are specific to the workplace. As a result, they provide little illumination on the guiding question of this book: How do talented young people become, or fail to become, good workers?

An Investigation of Good Work

The following three chapters present the results of a multifaceted study of young people, between the ages of approximately fifteen and thirty-five, who were embarking on careers that would inevitably entail many situations and decisions with an ethical dimension. We will look at the ethical issues that they confronted or could expect to confront, and the considerations they brought to bear in negotiating such delicate situations. Necessarily and revealingly, this study cuts across the aforementioned issues of expertise, ethics, and work. Because it draws on a broader survey of good work in turbulent times, we will begin with a brief sketch of that umbrella study.

Professions have developed over the years as a means of providing needed and desired services to the surrounding community.[15] In modern developed societies, professionals are accorded a certain degree of status and autonomy in return for providing valuable services to the lay public and behaving in a disinterested rather than a selfish manner. The best-known example, of course, is the profession of medicine. In taking the Hippocratic Oath, physicians pledge to do no harm, to come to the aid of the sick and the infirm, to avoid corruption, to use appropriate healing techniques, and the like. In return for adhering to such an admirable creed, they have long occupied an honorable place in the community. By the same token, lawyers are charged with ensuring justice and fair treatment for their clients; teachers pass on knowledge to their students and prepare them for an uncertain world; and analogous bargains are forged in various other fields of endeavor.

Professions and professionals encounter a great many pressures. It may happen that once-adequate expertise ceases to suffice; that other individuals or institutions develop a comparable ability to provide the same services; or that practitioners forget their core mission and are seduced by other rewards or goals.[16] To remain with the example of medicine: the emergence of new technologies can change practice dramatically (more tests, fewer regimens of aspirin and bed-rest); new institutions such as managed-care facilities can alter the relation between physician and patient (for instance, by mandating length of appointments and treatments); and physicians may enter the profession in order to become wealthy rather than to serve those in need of medical care. Usually, these pressures can be withstood as a "righting mechanism" comes into place. For example, many physicians have successfully resisted pressures from health maintenance organizations (HMOs) to withhold information about costly treatment options. But at times, forces—whether from within the profession or from without—are sufficiently powerful that the profession itself is sent reeling; whether the profession will recover, or be replaced by some other institution or line of work, remains uncertain. For example, the practice of surgical bloodletting by barbers was eventually replaced by science-based medicine; litigious lawyers may one day be replaced by professional mediators; live classroom teachers may someday be supplanted by distance learning involving remote persons or pure computational instruction.

In the United States over the past few decades, market forces have had the greatest impact on the professions.[17] Spiraling expenditures for medical care have resulted in the creation of HMOs, which are charged with keeping costs under control and, in many cases, with generating profits for shareholders. Not infrequently, physicians end up clashing with the managers of HMOs because the Hippocratic priorities may be at odds with financial considerations. Nowadays scarcely any profession is insulated from such strong market forces. Many lawyers work for huge multinational corporations that are under constant pressure to increase their "billable" hours and earn greater profits. Market forces have even entered the educational realm. They can be seen in operation in all sorts of arenas: colleges freely advertise in the "marketplace" of students, and primary and secondary schools that permit advertising in their halls and offer admission to students with vouchers.[18] Newspapers and television stations compete for audiences that are needed to sustain news as a lucrative "profit center" of the "entertainment business."[19] And in the United States, where patronage is rarely unrestricted, both scientists and artists, in various ways, must please their respective markets if they are to secure the money they need to carry out the work of their choice.[20]

The goal of the research program described here was to determine how individuals who wish to perform good work—work that is both excellent in quality *and* responsible to the broader society—can succeed in doing so at the present time. Market forces today have unprecedented power; there are few counterforces (religion, ideology, family) of comparable influence, and people's sense of time and space is being altered by technological innovations such as the World Wide Web. Though the problem of how to carry out good work is multifaceted and ever-present, our own investigation looks especially closely at market forces because of their extraordinary power on the contemporary scene in the United States and, increasingly, around the world.

A word on the word "profession." One can define "profession" narrowly, including only those careers—such as law or medicine—that require specific training and licensing. The definition we use here is broader. It encompasses any career in which the worker is awarded a degree of autonomy in return for services to the public that are performed at a high level. According to this definition, it is within the power of the individual worker to behave like a professional, should she or he choose to do so.

The first three professions selected for study were journalism, genetics, and theater. While one can make an argument for studying nearly any set of professions, these three turn out to be especially important and intriguing today. Journalists inform the public about what is going on in the world; to borrow a term from the biologist Richard Dawkins, they supply mental "memes"—the units of information that circulate among human beings, such as stories, jokes, and rumors.[21] Geneticists explore the basic units (genes) and laws of human life; for the first time in history, they are discovering procedures that could alter the heredity of this generation and its descendants. Individuals who work in theater are artists; more so than other artists, professionals in theater deal concretely and specifically—via live performances—with issues of human life, both real and imagined. By focusing on the essential matter of these three fields—on memes, genes, and scenes, one might say—one gains insight into our own nature as human beings. Moreover, the lessons learned can readily be applied to other professions, ranging from the visual arts to veterinary medicine.

This study is based on lengthy in-depth interviews with leaders and creators in these and other professional domains (see the Appendix on Methods for more detail). We asked the participants to provide information on many topics: their goals, their guiding principles, the obstacles and opportunities they encountered, the strategies they used, the people who had influenced their work lives, the changes that were taking place in their professional area, their hopes and fears, their treasured values, and the "moves" that they would make when faced with ethical dilemmas—hypothetical, as well as ones reported from their own experience. We transcribed the interviews and then analyzed them in great detail in an effort to find patterns within and across the various professions.[22] We also secured background information about the participants, which we used, along with data from nominators and other sources, to evaluate the veracity of their testimony.

As researchers, we listened sympathetically to the testimony of every participant but did not check our skepticism at the door. Though the project aimed to identify and understand the most exemplary workers, one cannot know for sure who is or is not a good worker—if, indeed, the world can be so readily dichotomized. But we *were* able to identify the constituents of good work and to observe how it is practiced, or how it could be practiced, by experts currently working in various domains. And as we gained a better understanding of the nature and provenance of good work, we began to work with groups involved in the education of young workers.

A Study of Veterans: Alignment and Misalignment in the Professions

Our study of good work among veteran professionals yielded a number of robust findings. Perhaps not surprisingly—since they were nominated by colleagues as workers at the peak of their respective professions—most of our participants spoke of their calling in lofty terms. The scientists in the study wanted to pursue knowledge openly, share their findings, and contribute to the general welfare of humankind. The journalists wanted to cover the most important current events fairly and in detail, so that their readers and viewers would be well informed about the state of the world. The theater professionals sought to entertain and educate audiences, and expose them to classical works as well as contemporary plays.

But the ease with which these workers could achieve their goals differed markedly, according to the circumstances in each field. The geneticists were the most fortunate. At the time they were interviewed, in the late 1990s, their field was *well aligned*—that is, everyone with a stake in that profession wanted the same things, roughly speaking. People all across the globe were—and still are—looking to geneticists for the biological secrets that will enable humans to live longer and healthier lives. And so the general public, the shareholders in biotechnology companies, and scientists in other fields were cheering these researchers on to important discoveries and crucial applications.

Journalism, in stark contrast, was a poorly aligned profession. Most of the journalists interviewed described themselves as frustrated by their work. Nowadays, most news outlets—whether print or broadcast—are owned by large multinational corporations. Rarely are these corporations managed by individuals with a personal knowledge of or dedication to journalism. Executives tend to see the news as simply another profit center in a highly diversified corporation. For their part, current audiences do not exhibit much interest in comprehensive and well-rounded reports of complex worldwide phenomenon. They seem to crave news that is easy to digest, sensationalistic, and of personal interest; as the saying goes in the news business, "If it bleeds, it leads." This congeries of circumstances yields a profession that is demoralized. Most of the journalists interviewed for this study said they did not feel they could practice their craft as they would have liked; and, unlike the geneticists, many were considering leaving the profession.

Given how hard it is to make a living as a professional actor, one might well ask why someone would choose theater as a career. The participants in our study displayed surprising unanimity on this topic: they were attracted to theater from an early age and had difficulty envisioning a life in any other pursuit. They were willing to put up with many hardships, even take unappealing part-time jobs, just so they could have the excitement of performing live in front of (hopefully) appreciative audiences. Monetary rewards figured little in their calculations. Yet they differed in their assessment of theater's future viability, and the extent to which theater could avoid what more than one disparagingly termed "Disneyfication." They did not necessarily recommend the theatrical calling to anyone else; in fact, most encouraged young people to go into other professions if they could. But they expressed few regrets about their own personal choices. Even if theater was not particularly well aligned as a profession, the individuals we surveyed felt satisfied with their career decision.

On the surface, then, it appears that individuals are well-advised to select professions in which they—if not the profession as a whole—feel aligned. Yet the overall picture that emerges is more complex. For one thing, alignment proves to be a temporary state of affairs. In the early twentieth century, physics was a very well-aligned science. But after atomic bombs were detonated over Japan, that alignment was rapidly lost; important decisions about research became the province of politicians instead of scientists. (Professionals in the natural sciences used to display physics-envy; nowadays, physicists admit to bio-envy.) In the mid-twentieth century, U.S. journalism—in contrast to its present state—seems to have been quite well aligned. There was great admiration for CBS News under the leadership of journalist Edward R. Murrow, and similar respect for the major publications associated with Henry Luce *(Time, Life)* and Gardner Cowles *(Look).* In the field of genetics, the current alignment could easily become attenuated or destroyed in the wake of some major mishap—a kind of genetic Chernobyl or Three Mile Island. Moreover, after the terrorist attacks of September 11, 2001, the status of both journalism and genetics was altered, at least temporarily: high-quality journalism became more greatly prized, while funding for basic research in science was threatened.[23]

Not only is alignment temporary, but sometimes it is not even desirable. Apparent alignment may mask underlying problems that require attention. For example, the current alignment in the biological sciences may result from the fact that practitioners are unaware of—or unconcerned by—the extent to which research decisions are being dictated by financial considerations rather than scientific ones. In the early 1990s, most basic research was supported by the government and vetted by peer review. Today, research is increasingly supported by biotechnology companies, which are underwritten by venture capitalists; and eventually these companies have to turn a profit. By the same token, the absence of alignment in a profession may have positive facets. The very fact that journalism at present is poorly aligned can serve as a stimulus for idealistic journalists. It may impel them to embrace the heart of their craft and to inspire their colleagues to do likewise. Indeed, in our project we identified a number of initiatives in journalism—for example, the foundation-supported Committee of Concerned Journalists—that placed the ideals of the profession at the very center of current activities. Similarly, efforts to keep theater vigorous, engaged, and energized have been initiated by organizations like the

Bread and Puppet Theater and the Underground Railway Theater. The relative dearth of comparable idealistic enterprises in the realm of genetics could be a cause for concern.

Once our research on the professions was well launched, we began to wonder about the origins of good work—a natural question on the part of developmental psychologists. Participants in midlife can provide retrospective testimony and relevant anecdotes, but it is preferable to study individuals who themselves are in the process of becoming workers to determine the factors that influence the quality of their work in the present era. Given the choices we made with our study of veteran workers, we decided to look at young people who had already made a significant commitment to work in these same three domains. We ultimately surveyed two cohorts in each domain: a group of secondary school students (roughly fifteen to eighteen years of age) and a group of young adults (ages twenty to thirty-five) who were enrolled in professional school or had begun their first jobs. Details of our procedures are given in the Appendix on Methods and in the following three chapters.

Our Conceptual Framework

Until now, we have described our study with a minimum of theoretical and conceptual baggage. Indeed, since this is a fledgling effort in a new area of study, there is much to be said for proceeding largely in an empirical vein. Yet in the course of our work we have arrived at a framework that has guided our thinking and our analysis.[24] We will focus here on three separate spheres, which we term "domain," "field," and "person."

THE DOMAIN

We employ the term "domain" to refer to the long-standing mission and goals that have evolved in a professional realm. For example, in science, the term designates a specific set of aims and aspirations: to observe the world accurately, to develop appropriate theories and concepts, to carry out experiments carefully, to replicate the results, to report findings publicly, and to debate their significance. In journalism, the tenets of the domain include a commitment to a fair and carefully documented portrayal of events and individuals, along with a willingness to correct the record as warranted. In theater, the domain stresses well-prepared and skillfully executed performances, an authentic stance toward material and the character, preservation of important works, and so on. Domains—and their central missions—coalesce over many years and change very gradually.

THE FIELD

In contrast to the temporally persisting domain, the field consists of the set of institutions and individuals that happen to constitute a domain at a particular historical moment. Fifty years ago, the field of genetics comprised a small number of university-based biologists who carried out studies with relatively little financial support. Nowadays, the field contains thousands of researchers, many of whom work on multi-million-dollar projects in both public and private settings. Fifty years ago, the field of journalism in the United States consisted primarily of hundreds of independent newspapers and a few major radio and television networks. Today, it includes not only radio, TV, and newspaper companies but also the World Wide Web and a dizzying array of cable television stations. Most outlets are now owned by large multinational corporations that may have little personal stake in the quality of news coverage. Changes in theater as a profession are less salient. Among the trends one could mention are: the skyrocketing production costs and ticket prices, the rise of repertory companies, particularly in university towns, and the far greater opportunities for actors to perform on television.

The Person (or Self)

Since our data come principally from interviews, our attention necessarily falls on the individual as an active, reflective agent. In describing the "person" or "self" of the worker, we determine as much as we can about background, expertise, personality, temperament, beliefs, and values. To complement this portrait of the *enduring characteristics* of the person, we also probe for *key experiences,* especially ones that the individual considers transformative.

Each person is involved in the following relations:

1. Relations to other individuals (parents, friends, siblings) who play an important role in the person's development.[25]
2. "Vertical" relations at work. We include here relations to teachers, mentors, supervisors, anti-mentors (individuals who serve as negative role models) and paragons (individuals who are not personally known but who have inspired the young worker).
3. "Horizontal" relations at work, meaning the person's relations to peers at the workplace. These relations can be competitive, cooperative, or a blend of the two.
4. The person's relation to his or her own value system. Crucial here is the extent to which the person is able to live up to those values and beliefs that he or she deems most important.

While not dictating what we did, these concepts guided our procedures, our methods of analyzing the data, and the ways in which we present our findings. We asked our participants about themselves, their relations to others, their understanding of the domain, and their reactions to the current institutions and personnel in their field (see the Appendix on Methods). Some of our questions pitted these spheres against one another: for example, in asking participants about their sense of responsibility, we were asking them to explore whether they felt more responsible to specific individuals, to the domain, or to their own personal value system. Similarly, in posing ethical dilemmas to participants, we were asking them to pit the long-standing values of their domain against the more transient pressures and influences of the field.

Most of the questions undergirding our research—for example, those having to do with changes in the domain or with the characteristics of young workers—could be posed directly to our subjects. But three of them—which we term the "overarching questions"—can be answered only by doing comparisons across our various sources of data. The three overarching questions deal, respectively, with differences across the three domains (journalism, biological science, theater); differences across the three age groups (high school students, young professionals, veteran professionals); and the optimal steps toward encouraging good work among the young. Our specific questions, grouped according to focus, can be found in the appendix.

As a means of presenting our findings, we have created three vignettes in each professional sphere. As we saw in the case of the journalist Bill, the person is placed in tension with figures in a vertical or authority hierarchy. In the second case, as epitomized in the case of the geneticist David, the self is in tension with co-workers. In the third instance, exemplified by the young actor Martha, the self must resolve tensions of moral identity that are felt internally. We go on to discuss the factors that, individually or jointly, determine the quality of the work executed by the young professional. These factors reflect all three of the constituents—person, domain, and field—described above. Likewise, our concluding recommendations for the fostering of good work, and for determining whether it has taken place, draw on our conceptual framework.

Expectations and Uncertainties

Our study is avowedly exploratory. Most of the territory that we surveyed was unknown to us, and will probably be unfamiliar to most researchers and educators. Moreover, we are aware of clear limitations to our study: it is based primarily on self-reporting; our participants are drawn from a single region of one country; and, in the absence of longitudinal data, we are unable to disentangle age effects from cohort effects (for example, differences between subjects born in 1940 and those born in 1980). To be sure, we had a set of questions and an organizing framework, both introduced in the preceding pages. But it would be both misleading and grandiose to suggest that we had either a formal model or specific hypotheses to test. Our study will be a success if it leads to these more precise kinds of formulations.

We were particularly keen to identify the factors that most powerfully differentiate among our participants with respect to the dependent variables of interest—for example, participants' attitudes toward work, their sense of responsibility, or their ethical sensibility. One possible factor is their membership in a specific age cohort: perhaps all high-achieving secondary-school students are alike. Another is the nature of the domain: perhaps, irrespective of age, all journalists share more resemblances with one another than they do with either geneticists or actors. A third might be the current operation of the field: if, for example, market forces are dominant in some professions and not others, perhaps those forces will prove decisive in determining attitudes and behaviors. A fourth could be the peculiar circumstances surrounding young workers: for example, young journalists work in the protected sphere of the high school newspaper, while young geneticists are already apprenticed in competitive university-based laboratories. We did not have strong expectations in this regard.

When it came to specific measures, we did have some expectations. We thought that younger participants would be mostly concerned with themselves and with the individuals closest to them: family members and teachers. They would also feel most responsible to these individuals and would remain relatively naïve about the nature of the domain and the field in which they had recently become engaged. As they entered the professions, they would continue to feel responsible to those close to them, but they would also begin to feel a broader sense of responsibility to the workplace and to the profession they had joined.

With regard to another set of measures, we thought that the values cherished by participants would reflect their own current understanding of the domain. So, for example, high school actors might see theater as a way of gaining success and fame, while older actors might place a higher value on understanding themselves and the world. We also thought that the value profiles would reflect the current state of the field. So, for example, if competitive pressures were becoming increasingly acute in the area of genetics, younger participants might place a higher premium on achieving financial and job security.

The major impetus for our entire study was a desire to understand how young workers "in progress" confront—or fail to confront— ethical dilemmas that ordinarily arise on the job. One possibility is that young workers are extremely idealistic; if so, then they would exhibit the highest ethical standards compared to other age groups and show the most uneasiness when ethical limits were being tested. Another possibility is that the general ethical standards in some or all of the professions are declining, and that younger participants will be less ethically oriented, more likely to cut corners. We were not prepared for the more complex picture that emerged in the ethical sphere: many participants had a well-defined sense of "right" and "wrong" but felt they had the right, while they were still young, to cut corners in order to advance their careers.

One could no doubt come up with many other expectations and uncertainties. But there is no further need to speculate. In the following chapters we present the background for each profession, and then reveal what we actually found.

2

From Cocoon to Chaos in Journalism

Afree press is most appreciated where it is least available. When totalitarian regimes seize power, the first thing they do is to make sure they have control over the reporting of the news. Sometimes this takeover is dramatic: printing presses are smashed and broadcast studios are shut down. At other times, it is more subtle: in an Orwellian state, citizens do not even know that their minds are being manipulated. At still other times, the loss of a free press can be inadvertent: the owners of news organizations may simply place profits first, or the members of the press may come to value money or fame or job security over fair and full coverage.

Citizens of the United States are fortunate. Their country has had a free press for most of its history, and they have come to take it for granted. Two factors have been primary in the establishment and maintenance of a free press: the U.S. democratic form of government and the gradual professionalization of journalism. Thomas Jefferson famously commented, "Were it left to me to decide whether we should have a government without newspapers or newspapers without government, I should not hesitate a moment to prefer the latter."[1] Despite a press that was overtly partisan throughout much of U.S. history, the nation's democratic institutions have helped to ensure a variety of points of view. Perhaps reflecting the process of democratization, pressures for sensationalized reporting have also been evident throughout the country's history. Indeed, Jefferson himself was subjected to scurrilous and often baseless journalistic attacks during his political career.

At the start of the twentieth century, wealthy families began to buy newspapers; the Ochses and later the Sulzbergers acquired the *New York Times,* for example, and the Taylors became the owners of the *Boston Globe.* Seeking a wide audience, these families aimed to provide readers with a relatively unbiased and less sensationalistic account of the news.[2] To be sure, such family-owned papers were not beyond criticism—they had their preferences and their peeves. Yet the late twentieth-century shift to ownership by corporations—whose executives lack journalistic training and are more concerned about the bottom line than about quality news reporting—may well have contributed to the current roiled condition of the domain.[3]

As part of the Progressive movement in the early twentieth century, various efforts were launched to professionalize the domain. The process included the founding of journalism schools and professional organizations as well as the formulation of several codes of ethics, such as the one drawn up by the American Society of Newspaper Editors in 1923.[4] Several subsequent attempts were made to delineate ethical standards of conduct, and these codes have served as benchmarks by which to judge journalistic practices.[5]

The trends toward professionalization have had to contend with technological innovations and with the demands of the marketplace. The emergence of new technologies dramatically changed the ways in which journalists approach their work. The advent of radio and television necessitated new reporting methods and engendered sharp criticism regarding undue market influences and sensationalized reporting.[6] With each technological innovation, news became accessible to more people more quickly, and reporters' standards risked being compromised as they competed for an ever-widening audience. Pressures to speed up the news process have resurfaced in full force with the growing popularity of the World Wide Web as an information source.

Criticism of the press has been another constant in U.S. history. Today some critics charge that the news does not adequately represent the diversity of positions and peoples within the United States. Others accuse the press of having a leftist or "progressive" bias, while still others believe that nonmainstream views are systematically excluded, especially during times of war.[7] Some observers also claim that in today's "mixed-media culture" journalists rely increasingly on commentary, anonymous sources, information recycled from the Web, and an overly flexible set of journalistic standards.[8]

Introducing the Veterans

As part of our comprehensive "core" study, we interviewed sixty-one veteran journalists throughout the United States, the majority of whom worked in print or broadcast journalism (see the Appendix on Methods). Many were drawn to journalism because of their curiosity and their need to question everything around them. For example, the *Washington Post*'s star investigative reporter, Bob Woodward, spoke of his high school experiences as a janitor in his father's law firm:

> I guess I worked there two or three years, at nights and on the weekends. I looked at all the files and eventually made my way to the attic, where they had all the disposed files of all the cases in my small town. My father, a small-town lawyer, was a kind of revered figure who handled lots of problems for people. I discovered and looked up the divorce cases

of my friends, and cases about the mayor, and about other figures in town—this small town. And it was stunning that there was this sense in the town that everything is fine and everyone—simply put, everyone had a secret, or that there was a tax case, or some case, or something, not awful or untoward, but showed a gap between the public notion of who these people were and who they really were as revealed in the disposed files. So you see that as a young person, and it sears itself into your brain as a truth that probably would apply to other institutions in town. I was in the Navy during the Vietnam War; in the last year I worked in the Pentagon, and it was so clear, from my personal experience on the ship off the coast of Vietnam and what I saw, that the gap between what was being said publicly and what was really happening was so wide, just like the "disposed files."

Veteran journalists also believed that they had other qualities that were critical to their success as journalists—for example, a special talent for expressing themselves through the written word or the ability to identify with others. Laura Pappano, freelance writer and contributor to the *Boston Globe* and *The Commonwealth,* explained:

I think one thing is that I feel like I can walk into anybody's house and have something to identify, have something in common with them. . . . And then when it comes to hearing other people's stories, I really feel that I have a lot of empathy. When I was in Brockton [Massachusetts], sitting at this kitchen table, this seventeen-year-old girl and single mother and three kids sleeping in one bed—I mean, I really felt that it wasn't that different from me, in some ways. And almost everyone I've ever met, I've felt like there were some experiences or qualities that were not that different from mine.

In the eyes of these veteran journalists, their calling had three main purposes which shaped their own professional goals. Almost half of the individuals that we interviewed believed that their primary objective was to inform the public about events that were relevant to and might bring about change in their readers' lives. When asked how he judged his articles of which he is most proud, for example, Anthony Lewis, then a columnist at the *New York Times,* remarked:

> I actually do [think articles on Bosnia were important], because I think it *did* make a contribution, and it significantly, within journalism, helped to build the pressure that eventually led Clinton to do something. . . . It made some difference, and so I value that. . . . I'm proud of the stories that won the [Pulitzer] prize. . . . Not for the prize, but because they saved somebody's life.

Echoing Jefferson, almost as many journalists cited the need to support democracy. Journalists, they felt, provide readers with information that will allow them to engage in intelligent debate, and establish a forum for the free exchange of ideas. Noel Don Wycliff, editorial page editor at the *Chicago Tribune,* stated that "in a democracy, for people to remain free, they have to have knowledge, and somehow I'm a part of that chain." Frances Moore Lappé, a veteran writer and activist, cofounded a wire service to help "redefine what the media consider to be news" because "the kind of democratic social change that we believe is necessary for a fully functioning democracy, which really likes serving society, can't exist unless many, many more people are themselves involved in public life."

A third goal expressed by several veteran journalists was the empowering of disenfranchised minorities. Indeed, as confirmed by our value-sorting task, more than one-third stressed the importance of social concerns in their work. Reporters can help make public the issues and positions of minorities, so that members can unite around such perspectives. When asked about a series of articles she had written on gay individuals, Laura Pappano replied:

> There are a couple of things I feel proud about. That one, yes, because I knew that it was something that people there didn't want to hear, and yet there are a lot of people who are really suffering because they were made invisible. And sometimes I do believe that part of the role of a journalist is to give people who wouldn't necessarily be heard a chance to be heard and to have their voices be there, alongside President Clinton's. And whoever else. So I felt proud of being able to let those people tell their stories and have them be listened to.

The veteran journalists cared passionately about the truth and fairness of their work. They strove to create truthful, balanced, and accurate depictions of events. They saw themselves as demonstrating loyalty to their sources, the stories' subjects, and their readers. When asked what work he was most proud of, Tom Brokaw, long-time television news anchor at NBC, explained:

> I don't have a personal agenda. . . . I often tell people who worry that we're biased that that's the quickest route to failure that I know of. The audience is very perceptive about that, and when they think that you're trying to impose your views on them, they're not much interested in that. They're trying to get someone they can trust to kind of give them a fair idea of what happened that day, or what's likely to happen. . . . And at the end of this long period of time of being out there in the middle of all that, people still trust my judgment and are willing to get their information from me. And

have, by all of our measurable standards, faith in my integrity. I suppose that, more than any other single act, is something that I'm proud of. . . . In the television business, there's
no hiding from it. You're out there and they measure it every
week. A lot of folks get a vote, and you know where you
stand.

But despite these high standards for journalism and for themselves,
the veteran journalists were finding it increasingly difficult to uphold
the standards of the domain. Indeed, in striking contrast to the picture we obtained in other professions, more than half of the veteran
journalists spoke about changes in the news media as negative; the
remaining half were divided between those who saw the changes as
positive and those who found them neutral. Asked to rank their own
values, few veterans cited "Enjoyment of the Activity / Intrinsic Motivation." The journalists were particularly concerned that corporate executives tended to make decisions based on profits, and at the expense
of quality journalism. For example, travel budgets were being cut,
news staff was being downsized, and marketing departments were exerting undue influence on the types of stories to be printed.

In addition, newly emerging twenty-four-hour cable news stations
and news-oriented Websites were pressuring journalists to produce
stories faster than their competitors, and to make their copy ever
sexier. As a result, articles were often printed before all facts could
be confirmed, and reporters felt pressured to produce highly sensationalized stories. Bob Woodward voiced his concern:

Instead of worrying about the educational system in the Dis-
trict of Columbia, for instance, [what] all the reporters are
worried about is whether the mayor has a new girlfriend, or
is buying cocaine—relevant questions, but the city services
as you know them collapse. It's pot-hole city, and schools

don't work, and the police aren't there. What effort—how many reporter hours go to those subjects? . . . There is a scandal press corps.

Despite these fears, the veteran journalists enjoyed the practical advantage of having much more control over their work, and many were sustained by memories of a "golden age" of journalism—for example, the era of Edward R. Murrow at CBS News in the 1950s. On the other hand, high school, college-age, and young professional journalists were being indoctrinated into the domain in a time of rapid change, enormous pressures for speed and sensationalism, and little formal mentoring. Their position as novices within the domain further compounded the challenge of carrying out good work.

Young journalists now entering the professional workplace encounter challenges and pressures—as well as opportunities—that scarcely existed for previous generations of reporters. Though recent graduates continue to flood the market, employment rates in traditional news media have declined in recent years and are not expected to rise in the foreseeable future. These conditions reflect the emergence of nonprint media (such as the Web) and advances in automated printing technologies (such as desktop publishing). In addition, large-scale corporate mergers, declines in newspaper circulation, and increased reliance on freelance reporters have further slowed the growth of full-time employment opportunities.[9]

Journalism traditionally has been considered a stressful occupation, but the proliferation of real-time news sources has raised stress to peak levels. The new generation of reporters must be poised to capture late-breaking stories even when they occur at the end of a twelve-hour workday. As a result, journalists work long and unpredictable hours, and broadcasters are often left little time to prepare their programs. A young reporter at the *Boston Globe* described her work this way:

I think it's exhausting, more exhausting because of this twenty-four-hour news cycle and because of this daily [crunch]—especially at a daily newspaper or daily television news station that's putting something out every day. There's constant pressure to beat whoever else is trying to get this story. There is constant pressure to get little, tiny smidgens of things that other news outlets aren't going to be reporting. And there's constant pressure, I think, to make sure that what you're writing or producing is the best that you can write or produce in a short period of time.

This hectic and demanding lifestyle probably contributes to the high turnover rate. Some journalists find that their jobs do not easily accommodate families or personal lives; they leave the profession for occupations such as advertising and public relations, which use related skills and offer somewhat more predictable hours and career paths— not to mention better pay. According to a survey conducted by the National Association of Broadcasters and the Broadcast Cable Financial Management Association, the median annual salary of a television news reporter in 2000 was $29,110 and those in the lowest tenth of the wage scale earned less than $16,540.[10] When a twenty-six-year-old reporter at the *Middlesex News* was asked about the challenges of her work, she responded: "The biggest pressure I face is paying my bills."

Despite these challenging conditions, the young journalists we interviewed subscribed to the long-standing domain values of accuracy and objectivity. Like their predecessors, they wanted to write fair and accurate articles. They knew that they had to maintain their integrity to gain the trust of readers and viewers and to avoid costly lawsuits. While advances in technology have made news more readily available to individuals from all walks of life, the new technical means probably also contribute to less thoroughly scrutinized and more highly sensationalized articles—and young journalists are least able to resist these trends.

Introducing the Young Journalists

The young journalists we interviewed—twelve of them in high school, twenty in graduate school or beginning their careers—were drawn to the domain for a variety of reasons. Many described an early interest and a precocious ability in writing. A twenty-two-year-old beginning reporter, for example, said: "I wanted to be a writer for as long as I can remember. And when I was little, from the time that I could first write I was always sort of scribbling. In sixth grade, I actually wrote an entire novel (quote, unquote) based on friends and activities at school." Often, their talents were identified and encouraged by important people in their lives. A one-year resident staff reporter at the *Boston Globe,* for example, told us how her interest in writing originated: "I always liked to write, and I could write well. . . . And so, in the sixth grade, one of my teachers knew that I liked to write, so she asked if I wanted to write a column for the community newspaper. . . . So that's how I got my interest. And I kept it the rest of middle school, high school, college."

For others, writing helped express and contain emotion. Particularly when they were enduring difficult times in their childhood, such as parental divorce or alienation from peers, journalists discovered that through the written word they could express thoughts and feelings in a socially acceptable way. A young African American reporter for a major newspaper recalled, "I got to put a lot of thought into words. Things that I might not say or that I didn't think I could say well, I could write them."

Several high school journalists were attracted to the domain because of opportunities to meet other people and because of their admiration for individuals who already were involved in journalism, such as family members or previous editors of the school newspaper. Cub reporters were impressed by the key roles these individuals played in the community through their work as journalists.

Although pivotal early experiences drew journalists to the domain, other events shaped the ways they came to approach their work. Several journalists told us they had acquired habits of hard work and perseverance from their parents' examples and that these behaviors proved critical to their success thus far. An eighteen-year-old editor of his high school's newspaper, for example, described the effect of his father's belief that "hard work does have its rewards":

> I think of, again, my parents. I guess seeing my father work eighty hours a week and stuff like that. Hearing him come home at the end of the day and tell a success story, or something that went wrong, and how he wants to fix it. And especially when he would talk about when things went wrong at work. Obviously there are setbacks and things don't always go as he would please, and how he was going to deal with that made me realize that when certain things go wrong and things don't go as you want, don't give up, because there's a way to fix it if you really want to fix it.

Overall, the young journalists described themselves as hard workers who were highly dedicated to the endeavors they undertook. They were perfectionists who believed that things should be done correctly, and they did not tolerate errors in their own work or in the work of others. These young journalists also characterized themselves as good communicators, fond of telling stories as well as listening to the experiences and details of others' lives. A reporter at *Metro West Daily*, a newspaper in Framingham, Massachusetts, spoke of this passion:

I'm always fascinated with people telling stories, just the little details. I'm the kind of person who, [when] my grandfather used to sit around and tell these stories, and he'd be talking about how he had this blue tie back in 1942, and he used to wear it everyday, and everybody would think he was so boring, . . . I would be fascinated by the fact that he was fascinated with this blue tie. I thought that that was such a great detail. So I love just listening to people.

The journalists in our study were not particularly religious. If anything, they felt that the qualities that drew them to journalism kept them from uncritically espousing any set of beliefs or declarations. One young reporter said:

I'm Jewish, born Jewish, but I kind of consider myself agnostic. It's part of the "question everything." That is one of the sort of key components of being a journalist, is "question everything." Even if somebody tells you something, even if you trust them, question the source, question everything. I need proof that God exists, and I don't have it. . . . So there's been a lot of people who aren't very religious in the profession.

A word about the work lives of the two groups of young journalists with whom we spoke. The high school journalists were editors-in-chief of high school newspapers. Most had been involved with their newspaper for four years, beginning as reporters when they were freshmen, advancing to section editors during their sophomore and junior years, and achieving the editor-in-chief position during their senior years. They attended schools long reputed to have premier newspapers. Indeed, many individuals were invited to participate in our study because their papers had won prestigious national competitions such as the Columbia Scholastic Press Association award. These students learned most of their journalistic skills on the job, through trial-and-error as well as through contact with more experienced members of the team such as faculty advisors and former editors-in-chief. In addition, their work was highly collaborative. Many decisions—such as whether to print particular articles, the themes of specific issues, and the mission of the paper as a whole—were made jointly by the senior staff.

Our second group consisted of young professionals who had recently entered the work force. They were reporters in major metropolitan areas and worked for newspapers and broadcast stations that ranged from locally based to internationally recognized. In a pattern typical of the domain, the journalists had taken multiple pathways to obtain their positions. Many had followed a formalized route: working for high school and college newspapers, attending journalism school and participating in internships, and subsequently entering the domain as professional journalists. But others had pursued undergraduate majors in a variety of areas, such as history and political science, before entering the workplace. The latter groups believed that depth and breadth of knowledge provided the best foundation for a professional journalist; actual reporting skills could be learned on the job.

Whatever routes the journalists took to their first jobs, their workdays were consumed with certain regular tasks. They had to select the topics for their stories from an array of possibilities that could include local, state, national, and international events, and they had to establish criteria for determining which topics merited their readers' time and attention. Once articles had been selected, the journalists confronted another welter of possibilities regarding what to include in each article. Given space limitations, they had to sort through a vast amount of information and select the material which was most essential to the story. Yet there was another side to their job. Most of the journalists lamented that they also had to comply with their editors' demands regarding the types of stories to pursue and how best to obtain them. Those demands often created conflicts for the young professionals as they strove to perform their work in a responsible fashion.

As captured by the brief vignettes in Chapter 1, the young workers with whom we spoke confronted three kinds of tension. First, participants in the three domains encountered conflicts with authority figures such as editors, study and thesis advisors, theater directors, and parents. Second, they confronted difficulties with their peers and colleagues. Third, they experienced internal conflicts. These painful dilemmas often pitted the workers' personal ambitions against their responsibilities to others, or spurred them to think of cutting corners in their work in order to advance their careers.

Balancing Truth and Consequences: Tensions Faced by High School Journalists

The high school journalists we interviewed worked in highly cohesive and insulated settings. They reported on the events and issues in the school communities, whose members (including the young journalists) generally knew one another. The school setting afforded the fledgling journalists protection from many of the strains of professional journalism. They were not pressured to make a profit, for example, or to compete with other newspapers for readership. As such, they had greater liberty than most professional journalists to pursue the types of articles they wished to cover.

In their interviews, the high school journalists spoke of having two major missions. First of all, they felt an obligation to discuss topics that concerned their fellow students, such as tuition hikes, birth control, and suicide. Second, they believed that they should provide readers with information that would have a positive impact on their lives. And so they tried to celebrate school-related achievements—such as team victories—and avoid exposing individuals who had engaged in negative conduct. Such stories would damage individuals who were not buffered by anonymity and would threaten the cohesion of the school community.

As high school students, these aspiring journalists also had to deal with two kinds of adults. Faculty advisors supported their work and provided guidance about which stories should be pursued. Less happily, school administrators (perhaps in lieu of alumni or parents) often discouraged articles on controversial issues lest they reflect poorly on their academic institutions. Fledgling journalists—such as the young woman we'll call Sarah, whose story is told below—struggled to reconcile their responsibilities to the student body with their responsibilities to important authority figures in their lives.

DON'T ROCK THE BOAT (LIVING WITH AUTHORITY)

Sarah was editor-in-chief of a high school newspaper at a prestigious private school in the Northeast.[11] Though she realized that negative, and perhaps newsworthy, events did occur in her school, she felt it would be unfair to single out individuals or groups within such a tight-knit community. She knew that if she reported something negative about the football team, for example, everyone in the school would know precisely who was involved, and that she herself would probably encounter those students in the course of the school day.

> A lot of times, it's hard to know where to draw the line between reporting and being a community newspaper. And my concern is that, a lot of times, there's no sense in offending people. . . . I've never found a tremendous amount of value in doing that. . . . Yes, reporting on the winning goal or something is what we try to do. Things go wrong at [school], but I don't think—I've never seen a big reason for us to focus on that.

Sarah's goal of maintaining a positive focus in the newspaper was challenged by school members who did not share her mission. The paper ran a regular column entitled "Letters to the Editor." Students often wrote letters voicing grievances about individuals or school policies. Sarah recalled one instance in which a student wrote a letter complaining about a gay organization at the school. "We had one student—she wrote a column about being gay. Because we have a group at my school and it's supposed to be—it's the Gay-Straight Alliance. And she wanted to write a column about [how] she was sick of seeing it all over school because she thought it only involved gay people." Sarah had difficulty deciding whether to print such contributions. She felt an obligation to be a voice for the student body and an outlet for their concerns, but she worried that doing so would offend other members of her community.

While Sarah's principal goal was to target *positive* events occurring around campus, such as individual and team accomplishments, she occasionally sought to inform students about significant, though perhaps controversial, topics such as birth control and school violence. School administrators, however, questioned the appropriateness of printing controversial articles in the school newspaper. They often urged Sarah to let particular stories go unreported if they felt that those articles would reflect poorly on the school. In one instance, Sarah published an article about a series of rapes that allegedly occurred on school grounds; she did so because she believed that reporting the crimes was important for the safety of fellow students. The admissions office, however, opposed publication of the article and refused to buy its standard one hundred copies of that issue.

The conflicts Sarah experienced between her responsibilities to authority figures (such as the admissions officer) and those she felt to her readers were echoed in many of our interviews with high school journalists. A seventeen-year-old editor-in-chief at a prestigious private school described the time she was called into the headmaster's office to be reprimanded for including "inappropriate humor" in the newspaper. After that, she said, every time she made an editorial decision "I just think about myself in his office, thinking, 'Okay, could I be there?'" The young journalists we interviewed frequently cited a Massachusetts law prohibiting school authorities from censoring school newspapers, yet they were strongly influenced by school administrators' concerns. In fact, they invariably resolved this conflict by choosing not to print articles to which administrators were opposed.

Such intrusion into the editorial process may take place at the university level as well. In November 2002, Nick Will, a student at the Harvard Business School, resigned his position as editor-in-chief of *Harbus,* a campus newspaper. Some days earlier, the newspaper had published a satirical cartoon in which members of the school's career counseling office were portrayed as "incompetent morons." Will and his fellow editors were admonished to avoid "disrespectful language" and to "steer clear of all questionable content." In his statement of resignation, Will spoke of "personal intimidation or threats" by Harvard administrators. Officials at the school denied that they had threatened the editors. At the same time, they clearly were embarrassed that their actions were seen as sacrificing the value of a free press to the perceived need to avoid offending a group of employees.[12]

Though they felt compelled to comply with administrators, the student journalists with whom we spoke resisted pressure from often powerful and vocal peer groups. Indeed, young journalists actually strove to maintain the integrity of the subjects they were writing about. For example, when fellow students wanted to publicize the negative behavior of school members, the journalists actively worked to convey students' grievances while striving to preserve the self-respect of the people discussed in their articles. In addition, rather than just focusing on the particulars of the given issue, the young writers tried to construe negative issues as a means of catalyzing change and offering alternative solutions to problems. A seventeen-year-old high school editor explained that he was attempting to present these issues "in a way that isn't adversarial, but one that is just kind of expressing, giving a challenge."

In addition to listening to the experiences of these student journalists, we explored their lives in two other ways. First, we asked them point blank to whom they felt responsible. All of them claimed they felt responsibility to others—and they ranked "Understanding, Helping, or Serving Others" as one of the more important values. They said they would refrain from printing stories that would cause discomfort for members of their community. Well over half also expressed a responsibility to readers. In this respect, they differed from the older journalists we interviewed, who were more likely to say they felt responsible to their own personal values or the domain of journalism per se. Perhaps a stronger sense of responsibility to either the self or the domain would have strengthened the students' commitments to their readers when confronted by pressure from authority figures.

We also asked the high school journalists to complete an ethics survey. They were asked to rate their level of concern (no concern, some concern, or great concern) on a list of issues relating to the decision of reporting on a controversial story. Our prompt read as follows:

> Suppose a journalist of your acquaintance received a tip on a story concerning an incident from the private life of a public figure. Which of the following would raise an ethical issue or would cause moral concern, and why?
>
> 1. Reporting the story
> 2. Covering this story instead of covering a major international news story (e.g., a war in another country)
> 3. Reporting a story based on a tip from an anonymous source without additional confirmation

4. Airing this story first or putting this story on the front page

5. Presenting the story in a way that is both informative and entertaining

6. Presenting the story as a mixture of reporting and some form of commentary (e.g., analysis, opinion, speculation, narrative, or judgment)

7. Reporting the story even though it may affect the public figure's chance of receiving a fair trial

8. Reporting the story before all facts can be checked, in order to be the first to break the story

9. Shareholders or corporate owners deciding whether or not the story should be reported

Data from this survey support many of the conclusions drawn from our interviews. The students expressed great concern about the need to check the accuracy of the facts or about relying on an anonymous tip. At the same time, they were equally concerned about a decision that was made by shareholders or owners—perhaps reflecting their frustration with limitations set by the "shareholders" in their own settings (e.g., school administrators). Most of all, they stressed the dangers of printing a story that might affect a public figure's chances of receiving a fair trial; quite possibly, this response reflects their concern with exposing individuals in their school community. Overall, the student journalists emerged as individuals who wanted to do the right thing and were distressed by external forces that seemed to prevent them from behaving in a fair-minded way.

Young Professionals on the Move

Journalists embarking on professional careers said they wanted to write articles that would have a positive impact on the lives of their readers; in this respect they were like their younger counterparts and unlike the seasoned professionals, who generally spurned journalism aimed at serving the community. Several young professionals spoke of instigating change through their stories and informing readers of issues that could enhance the quality of their lives. A twenty-nine-year-old reporter, once an editor for a weekly town newspaper, claimed that journalism "almost becomes a way of life. A way of thinking, just a belief system in this, and it's somewhat idealistic, but sort of you're doing public good, you're providing information." She went on to say that "I feel like I have a mission, like I have a responsibility to the whole community." The twenty-two-year-old reporter at the *Boston Globe* stated: "Journalistically, I think I was interested in how . . . can I affect people in better ways?"

The professional journalists also believed that in order for their readers to make informed decisions, it was essential that their stories accurately portray the issues at hand. They strove to be objective in their reporting and to present all sides of an issue. When another young reporter at the *Boston Globe* was asked to whom she felt most responsible in her work, she replied: "The people that I'm writing about . . . the people that the issue impacts. And to myself. I feel I have a great need to be fair. And yet there's one side that clearly was wrong, clearly did something illegal or whatever. Their side has to be represented."

Where did the journalists acquire this sense of responsibility to others? Apparently not in graduate programs of journalism. Though "J school" gave them time to consider ethical dimensions, they reported that graduate school left them uninformed about the challenges they faced on a daily basis. The skills they needed to carry out their tasks as professional journalists, they said, were learned almost exclusively on the job, and classroom training was "a waste of time."

Still, some students in schools of journalism had inspiring teachers and mentors who gave them first-hand accounts of the power of journalism and conveyed a passion for the work. A young reporter recalled the impact of one of his professors:

> [He] had seen it all, and he told us about it. He told us what it was like to cover the White House when Richard Nixon was resigning. The day he was resigning, he said, they locked the doors in the pressroom. "And we had no idea what to expect," he said. "I'll never forget it. We expected the light bulbs to pop out of their sockets and gas to start seeping into the room," he said. The world had completely gone mad. Watergate was true. And it was those stories that made me say, wow, this is sort of a legendary life that you can lead. And not many people get there. But I mean, I just find that so inspiring. So [he] was sort of a role model of just how fascinating this career can be.

The journalism professors our subjects mentioned also stressed the importance of accuracy. They demanded high-quality writing from their students, and refused to tolerate oversights or mistakes such as spelling errors and misquotes. A beginning reporter recalled the influence of various teachers: "I think I've always kind of believed that [accuracy is important]. But—no doubt about it—it came from graduate school, from the professors that I had in graduate school."

Like their high school counterparts, the young professional journalists said they wanted to effect positive change in their readers. The working journalists, however, faced formidable challenges in trying to realize their goals. In contrast to the collaborative atmosphere in school, young professional journalists frequently described a lack of mentorship and an absence of collegiality in the workplace, particularly at large newspapers. A town reporter at the *Patriot Ledger* (published in Quincy, Massachusetts) described this frustration: "I guess one other thing is, I really would like it if people—an editor or someone, in any of the places I work—took the time to sort of be a little bit more concerned with you as a person. And I know that's something that's probably wishful thinking. But there tends to be a lot of, you feel like a number. A lack of an identity. . . . It's something that bothers me."

Rather than viewing the newspaper as a joint effort by staff, the journalists we spoke with considered it the product of a series of independent contributions—hence the sense of competition among colleagues that many described. In their experience, journalists vied with one another for the front-page story; for promotions to more prestigious positions, columns, and areas of coverage; and for the rights to stories that fell within the jurisdiction of two or more beats. According to the *Patriot Ledger* reporter, "There is definitely the small sense of competition that the people you are working with are the people that you're competing against for promotions in the future."

The intra-staff competition pushed journalists to seek out stories that would compel their readers' attention and advance their own standing within the news organization. Though they described themselves as "honest at heart" and frequently objected to editors' urgings to sensationalize articles, several journalists claimed they would use deceptive tactics to *uncover* a story. To understand this apparent contradiction between struggling to maintain one's journalistic integrity and a willingness to use questionable methods to attain "the front-page story," consider Karen, a young professional at a prestigious newspaper. Note that this scenario, in contrast to the others presented in this book, caused little tension for the professional involved. We need to understand why some journalists do *not* see their practices as riven with potential ethical conflict.

A Means to an End (Living with Others)

Karen was a young reporter at a well-respected newspaper in the Northeast. As an entry-level journalist, her primary source of competition came from summer interns who were recruited from elite undergraduate journalism programs. Karen was frustrated with editors who offered the interns privileges and choice assignments, even though she had more seniority:

> One of the things that I really learned from the interns that bothered me so much was that—it was my first company experience because [the newspaper], above everything else, is a big company—seeing how who you know is sometimes a lot more important than what you know. . . . To see these people come in, have the editor of our paper be taking them out to lunch, who's never even said hello to me. And I hated it. But looking back on this summer, it really, for me, really taught me the lesson of bad leadership and bad management. Because that's completely what I fault [the newspaper] for in this situation. . . . I really learned that you're going to be overlooked sometimes. That you're going to be—you're not always going to get the recognition that you deserve. . . . At other places I've worked, I've always sort of been the little young superstar. And there was never anyone else like me there. And now, all of a sudden, to have these people come in and see them sometimes getting better stories and working better shifts was really sort of a slap in the face.

Karen believed that competition could be "good for the soul." Some of her best work was born from the competitive atmosphere and her reluctance to be outdone by the interns. She began to work longer hours ("Most of them work about twelve hours a day, and so I would stay fourteen"), in the hope that she would be the one present to cover breaking stories. But this competitiveness had a downside. Karen described herself as honest and believed that "the cardinal rule of journalism is truth-telling." Yet her strong desire to provide readers with important information and to compete with other staff members compelled her to use questionable tactics to obtain her stories. For example, she misrepresented herself to others in order to get interviews. She did not, however, perceive such behavior as contradicting her goals of being truthful and honest. She argued that it was okay to use dishonest methods to get an honest story. In other words, the ends justified the means.

When asked if her goals of honesty and accuracy were shared by her colleagues in journalism, Karen replied:

> Yes, I do think so. Definitely accuracy, because I think that it would be tough for people to be drawn to journalism if they weren't drawn to some sort of sense of accuracy, because it's such a staple. Honesty is tough because journalism . . . is such a really—unfortunately—manipulative profession. So I think, in what they print, honesty is very important. But in tactics used to get what they print, I'm not sure that honesty is always so important. . . . There are a lot of times where journalists do dishonest things to get honest things.

As one example, Karen mentioned situations in which journalists used deceptive methods to reveal a county's "blatant racism." The journalists wanted to expose exactly how black people were treated differently from whites in certain communities, particularly when it came to buying cars and homes. And so they presented themselves to the car dealerships and real estate offices as potential buyers, rather than journalists, in order to get first-hand accounts of discriminatory behavior. Karen justified this deception:

> So I think that honesty is definitely—it's definitely something that I think people are, at heart, honest. But I think that tactics sometimes used are dishonest. I don't always think that dishonest tactics are used; they are mostly used for

good reasons. Those stories, the one on the racism, I mean
that was—that served the public good. I applaud what they
did in that case. . . . So I definitely think there are times for
dishonest tactics. And I can only speak on what I've seen,
and what I've seen in this small amount of print journalism
I've worked in, I would say that most people do have accuracy and honesty at heart.

Several of the other journalists we interviewed invoked similar means-
ends justifications. Early in an interview, one participant stressed the
importance of honest reporting. Accuracy, she said, "is inherent . . .
the key to the profession." But when asked if there was anything she
wouldn't do to get a story, the same journalist responded:

Absolutely wouldn't do? That leaves the door open for a
whole bunch of things that I *would* do. Committing a crime,
obviously, in the process of getting a story, you wouldn't. But
even that, I guess. I mean, if the story is that good . . . if you
hear somehow there's a secret governmental meeting going
on about the future of some air station, air base, and they're
not supposed to be holding this meeting because of open-
meeting law or whatever, and you find your way in there,
and you have to stick yourself into a closet—if you've got to
get the story, you've got to get it. . . . If you're in the right,
then it's okay to break laws.

Though the professional journalists with whom we spoke experienced little dissonance when they voluntarily engaged in questionable
practices to uncover breaking stories, they expressed a great deal of
distress when pressured by others to violate their integrity. Several of
the journalists were quite troubled when their editors urged them to

make the content of their stories less than truthful. As the proverbial low men on the totem pole, the reporters were expected to comply with their editors' demands even when this meant they had to compromise their personal goals and values. As a result, the professional journalists said they often had to choose between their career ambitions and their personal integrity. Reflecting a pattern that we observed across all three domains, *they themselves* wanted to be able to decide when to skirt important ethical principles. They had to negotiate ways to accommodate their editors' often improper demands without relinquishing their own standards and their own reasons for participating in the domain. The story of James, a young journalist at a well-known television station in the Northeast, illustrates such tensions.

DAVID VERSUS GOLIATH (LIVING WITH SELF)

James was a twenty-three-year-old white male who worked for a station we'll call Channel 3. As a freelance writer, he gathered information from Associated Press sources and local authorities to write news script, and located video footage from feeds and archives to edit them for stories. James had entered the professional workplace with lofty ambitions regarding his own career and the kind of uplifting human interest stories he wanted to provide for his audience. He strove to be positive when conveying news to a large audience. Whenever possible, he tried to add a hopeful note at the end of a sad news story.

Since his early days as a writer for Channel 3, however, James's producers had focused mainly on "negative stories"—those concerning murders, deaths, and scandals. When we spoke with him, the station had just aired fifteen continuous hours—with no commercial break—focusing on the fatal plane crash of John F. Kennedy, Jr., his wife, Carolyn Bessette Kennedy, and her sister, Lauren Bessette. James lamented, "News looks for everything that's negative, and it does it a lot." He was rarely able to pursue the types of touching and poignant stories that inspired his involvement in journalism, though he looked forward to a time when he might have greater control over his work. "Everyone is going to have their own opinion of what they think is the most important aspect of a story," he told us. "Pretty much what I think I'm doing now is I'm learning what are the most important things that will affect the most people. . . . I concede to the producers and the executive producers now because I understand I don't have the experience they have. Whereas five or six years down the road, I'll be more vocal about what I think, about what's the most important aspect of a story, or what I think the most people will benefit from hearing."

The producers at Channel 3 faced increasing competition from fast-paced media outlets such as twenty-four-hour cable news stations, radio stations, and the Web, as well as from local and national papers. In order to contend with competitors, news directors and producers were requiring broadcast reporters and writers to craft stories that would attract the attention of potential viewers. James was often pressured, for example, to focus on stories that would "win the ratings" and attract a greater "share" of viewers than other stations. He remarked that this stiff competition was just "another factor you have to think about in television."

In James's view, his producers were so driven by competition that they had become detached from the pain and suffering of the individuals who figured in the news reports. On one occasion, the station aired a tape of a woman who had recently learned that her child had died in a fire. James was uncomfortable with the "If it bleeds, it leads" approach:

> The news sometimes, I would say, oversteps its bounds.
> They sometimes cross the line. . . . Me, personally, I say,

"Wow, that really shouldn't have been on television." And sometimes, I'm watching it, and I'm like, "How did the producers let this go through?" . . . There's a fine line, because usually the video that's crossing a line is usually the best. . . . And a lot of times what happens is they don't have time to figure [it] out. . . . And we have to decide. It has to be an instantaneous decision: either we're going to run this or we're not. There's been a few times where I've said, "We shouldn't be running this." . . . Since I've been growing up, they [the producers] have been taking a little more liberty because it's all about ratings. They're losing market share every day. You've got to keep the viewers watching.

James spoke about journalists' responsibility to the public—their obligation to listen to audience feedback and to people's concerns about the appropriateness of particular stories and video footage:

I sit in the newsroom a lot after the show, and we get a lot of calls. Especially after we run either questionable material or we don't run something. There's a lot of "What happened to this?" "How come you're not reporting on this more?" The public is usually—they'll let you know if they didn't like something. . . . When that woman was on TV after her child died, the phones lit up. . . . It's the responsibility that we have to the viewer. This is something—we have to keep it within a framework of respectability.

In light of the demands to focus on more seductive stories that would increase ratings, James was reexamining his interest in journalism. He also realized that if he wanted a permanent position as a writer or broadcast reporter, he would have to move to an obscure location and write for a smaller market. Though the work at his station had doubled, the staff had been cut in half as a result of financial pressures, and James was receiving neither a full salary nor benefits.

> The things that surround the work . . . get frustrating. Pretty much right now television is scaling back, like local network television, in terms of budgetary concerns. . . . You're working really hard and they are scheduling you. I was there twelve, thirteen hours yesterday, but they don't want to work with you on the other end. . . . You're doing all this hard work, but there is no reward.

James's goals and frustrations were echoed by many of the journalists with whom we spoke. Several claimed that their desire to provide readers with truthful depictions of important events was undermined by editors who were more concerned with the bottom line than with upholding their societal and domain-related obligations. The journalists were often pressured to sensationalize articles and to cut corners in order to beat competitors in breaking news stories. A striking 90 percent of the young professional journalists in our study said they were distressed at having to interview grieving individuals. Though these demands often required journalists to violate their personal and journalistic integrity, they felt they had little choice but to comply with their editors' instructions. Failure to do so would have cost them, at best, the respect of their superiors and colleagues, and, at worst, their jobs.

The journalists contrived many strategies to resist problematic directives. Sometimes they devised methods to maintain their integrity within the bounds of their editors' requests; sometimes they defied their superiors outright; sometimes they simply complied. In cases where there was pressure to print an article before the facts had been checked, one twenty-two-year-old graduate student at Northeastern University had developed a particular strategy:

I guess you could say I've twisted the truth to an editor. Because if I don't want a story to run, I'll make up an excuse that I know that he'll accept, more so than "I want to double-check these facts." I'm not saying I'm lying to my boss. I'm just saying if you truly believe your story is not ready and you think that you're going to do more harm than good, you just figure out ways to get it not published. . . . Maybe I'll say that I want to double-check a quote because I don't think I got it right. He won't run a story if he thinks we're going to misquote someone.

Other reporters, when asked to interview individuals in mourning, lied to their editors and told them they couldn't get the interview or were otherwise unsuccessful: "I won't sell my soul for a story." A young reporter told us, "I think that there are deeper values. There's something deeper inside me, at least, that says, 'Enough is enough.'"

But usually journalists do what they're told, for fear of losing their jobs and their credibility in the workplace. They "stretch the truth" and interview those in mourning, to obtain more enticing stories; they print articles they consider unready for publication, in order to beat competing news sources. One young professional reporter received a tip: a residential facility for troubled youth was about to be accredited, though a resident had recently died under suspicious circumstances. The reporter was unable to confirm the circumstances of the story, because it was late in the evening and the accrediting agency could not be reached. When she consulted her editors, however, she was told to print the story so that their newspaper would not be scooped. "So we did that," the reporter told us. "I still thought it was irresponsible. I still thought I should have waited a day. But I did it, which I regretted."

The young professional journalists worried a great deal about cutting corners this way. To lessen their anxiety they focused on the future, when they would be likely to have the authority and status to refuse such tasks. They also shifted the blame, arguing that their supervisors established the rules and that they had little choice but to comply. Yet at the same time, they were willing to use some deception themselves to get a story. How did they reconcile these differences? How could they object to demands that they violate their integrity, while using dishonest tactics themselves? Apparently these young journalists judged their integrity not by the "road to hell" tactics that they used to get a breaking story, but rather by the merits of the piece and their ultimate "good intentions." Unable to pursue the literate and life-enhancing stories they had once dreamed of, they resorted to uncovering stories—regardless of the methods used—as a way of meeting their editors' demands and their own goals of providing readers with information that could impact their lives.

Navigating the Moral Minefield

For the most part, the young professional journalists described their responsibilities and reacted to ethical dilemmas in the same way the high school journalists did. Both groups emphasized the importance of accuracy, fairness, and balance. But the differences were instructive. Whereas the high school journalists stressed responsibility to others in their school, professional journalists emphasized their responsibility to readers—most of whom they presumably did not know. The young professional journalists did not exhibit a strong sense of responsibility to their workplace; indeed, only one third of them mentioned the workplace. They lamented the lack of mentorship and collaboration, and often looked forward to moving on to another site. In this way they differed both from the high school journalists, who felt a strong bond to their school community, and from the veteran journalists, many of whom felt a loyalty to the paper they had been with for many years.

The same disjunction was found in the relationship between individual and domain. While both the high school journalists and the veterans readily cited the classic mission of the domain, the young professionals—those reporters unprotected by school or by status and seniority—were equivocal. On the one hand, they spoke about journalistic integrity and the anxiety they felt when they were unable to pursue its mandates. They noted the increased competition that was forcing the domain to compromise its mission, and pointed to the sensationalism that was pervading contemporary journalism. In marked contrast to the veteran journalists, only 35 percent of the young professional journalists expressed a commitment to the domain. On the other hand, as manifested by their readiness to use unethical tactics, the young professional journalists seemed to lack a feeling of responsibility to the values of the domain. Such behavior suggests that the journalists were willing to compromise their own sense of journalistic integrity, or perhaps were uncertain how to make their way in a domain where the mission did not coincide with accepted practices. It is noteworthy that over half of the young professional journalists said that other persons, rather than they themselves, were responsible for the well-being of the domain.

The other feature that distinguished the young professionals was their explicit concern with ethical challenges. In their protective cocoon, high school students reported few daily challenges; and the senior journalists had presumably made their peace with any compromises they were making. In contrast, the young professionals readily chronicled the many dilemmas they confronted, the stresses they felt, and the strategies they developed to counter their editors' unrealistic demands. Several of them told us candidly about the deceptive methods they used—justifying them as a means of uncovering important information for their readers. We must add, however, that while the journalists may have been acting out of a sense of responsibility to their audience and a need to meet their editors' demands, such behavior also evidenced a betrayal of their readers' trust and a disregard for the individuals who figured in their stories.

A misalignment between journalistic ideals and journalistic daily practices, then, seemed to leave many young professional journalists with little meaning in their work. Indeed, they either lacked a sense of responsibility or felt that they were not permitted to uphold their responsibilities. Unlike the veteran journalists, who could at least remember a time in which the domain mission seemed more secure, entering professionals merely heard stories about the good old days of journalism. Such anecdotes were unlikely to sustain their faith in the domain. More than one-third of the young professionals in our study were giving serious consideration to leaving journalism for other careers, where they hoped to keep their integrity intact.

The alternative seemed equally bleak. Those who chose to remain in the profession might come to view current practices as acceptable—indeed, as the norm—as they permeate the domain. Indeed, we began to see evidence of this: some of the journalists admitted they used dishonest tactics as a way of accommodating their editors' demands. What will happen to the next generation of journalists? One young professional journalist poignantly described the dilemma he faced: "I think about leaving the profession just about every day. It depresses me. I think: Why am I doing this if I'm not getting what I want out of it? I sort of have this vision of something that's not really true. And that I'm sort of still clinging to these ideals that I had when I started out."

The young professional journalists completed the same ethics survey as the high school journalists, indicating their levels of concern about certain issues in journalism. One notable disparity between the high school students and the young professionals appeared on the issue of whether to "report on the story even though it may affect the public figure's chance of receiving a fair trial." A mere 8 percent of high school journalists but 30 percent of the young professional journalists said they would feel "no concern" about reporting this story. The relative indifference of the latter group probably reflected the buffer of anonymity enjoyed by professional journalists, who do not interact directly with their audience on a daily basis.

Differences and similarities also emerged between young professional journalists and the more seasoned veterans. The young professionals had mixed opinions about including both "entertaining" and "speculative" dimensions in the story. Furthermore, though we heard throughout our interviews about professional journalists' disappointment with the recent "dumbing down" of the news, they were actually divided about whether a story about the private life of a public figure should be aired on the "front page of a newspaper," possibly before "a major international news story."

Though the veteran journalists with whom we spoke did not specifically respond to an ethical survey, they mentioned several ethical concerns. They described some of their frequent "nightmares"—for example, that the news would come to incorporate more entertainment and that major international news stories would receive less coverage. They were troubled by the fact that audiences had developed an expectation for "lighter" stories rather than for news that was more complex but more important. Above all, they expressed dismay at being unable to pursue the domain's traditional mission, because corporate decisionmakers valued size of audience over quality of work.

As we consider the future course of journalism and journalists, we are struck by the contrasting experiences of the groups we studied. (In fact, we treated the two groups of young journalists separately in this chapter precisely because their experiences differed so dramatically.) In many ways, high school journalists led a charmed, indeed cocooned life. So long as they kept the wishes of authority figures in mind and did not directly besmirch the school's reputation, they enjoyed a great deal of freedom and a great deal of support from their peers and elders. The young professional journalists, however, worked in chaotic settings with little supportive mentoring. They were under the thumb of powerful editors whose desire to beat the competition all too often overshadowed the traditional journalistic values of fairness, objectivity, and responsibility to the audience. Nearly all the young professionals felt pressured to cut corners, sensationalize stories, and circumvent the dictates of higher-ups through one stratagem or another. In any event, few could unblinkingly state that both their ends and their means were honorable and responsible. They differed only in the extent to which they were disturbed by this crippling state of affairs.

If journalism is to remain a professional domain (rather than become a set of corporate profit centers), then the question of which individuals remain within the profession and how they behave as workers becomes crucial. It is entirely possible that the more idealistic young people will leave, and that those who stay will become ethically coarsened and more open to engaging in questionable practices. If so, the democratic ideals of earlier times and the professional goals of more recent times will recede from view. Yet it is also possible that the misalignment between the ideals of the domain and current practices in the field could motivate idealistic young professionals—or wise "trustees" of the domain—to bring about positive change. Should this be the case, then good work in journalism could become a happy commonplace.

3

The Long Windup in Genetics

IN 1999, TIME MAGAZINE DECIDED to select a Person of the Century. Prior to the appearance of the winner on the cover, the smart betting was on a political leader, such as Franklin D. Roosevelt, Winston Churchill, or even Adolf Hitler; or on a spiritual leader, such as Mahatma Gandhi, Martin Luther King, Jr., or Pope John Paul II. But when the choice of Albert Einstein was finally announced, many realized it was fitting. The twentieth century was as much a century of discovery, innovation, and creation as it was a century of wars, revolutions, and religious movements. And throughout most of it physics was the central science—the one that led, on the one hand, to an understanding of the most basic laws of the universe and, on the other, to the creation of technologies possessed of awesome constructive and destructive potential.

Science retains its importance today, but the torch of scientific hegemony long ago passed from the physical to the biological sciences. Quarter-century landmarks were the discovery of the structure of DNA—the molecule of life—in 1953; the first experiments in genetic engineering in the mid-1970s; and then, as the new century began, the completion of the successive drafts of the human genome.

In times past, scientists were often criticized and sometimes even jailed or burned at the stake for their beliefs. Nowadays we are more likely to award prizes to scientists than to persecute them for their discoveries. Yet—and here is a deeper reason for the selection of Einstein—we are keenly aware that those discoveries may have consequences that can in no way be anticipated. The study of genetics is not only yielding new data about the workings of the human body; it is also permitting the modification of foods and making possible new forms of biological and chemical warfare. Genetically derived drugs hold the promise of curing or alleviating dread diseases; yet these same drugs may have unexpected side effects and, in a few cases, may lead to unnecessary deaths. Society is now confronted with dilemmas about the fairness of genetic testing and the propriety of gene therapy. With the development of techniques such as the cloning of cells, tissues, and even entire organisms, society must ponder whether and how to control the ability to copy, create, and implant genetic material. But who represents society in these cases, and who ensures that discoveries will not be misused?

Genetics has also emerged as a lucrative field. Compensation in biotechnology firms is competitive and includes many incentives such as stock option plans and cash bonuses. Roughly three-quarters of biotech companies are privately owned; investors are lured by the windfall that can accompany the development of a successful drug. In the years 1993 to 2000, the biotech industry doubled in size. The amount of money invested in the U.S. biotechnology industry increased 156 percent in a single year, soaring from $137.9 billion in 1999 to $353.5 billion in 2000.[1]

As we noted with respect to journalism, market pressures are altering many domains, including the biological sciences. Scientists who work at biotechs often report to business managers who lack scientific training yet have the authority to approve or veto their recommendations. Although science has traditionally been an open pursuit, much current work is undertaken in secret until it is ready to be "launched" or made part of an initial public offering. Scientists who work in commercial settings typically have less autonomy than academic scientists, since the style and direction of research are most often dictated by market-driven considerations. Controversy will surely arise over the patenting of genes, a practice deemed essential by biotech companies who seek to protect the large financial investments entailed in developing gene-based products. This patenting practice can slow the pace of research, since scientists must obtain approval from the owners of specific genes. In a matter of a few decades, biotechs have forever altered our image of scientists as cloistered individuals who work chiefly for the joy of discovery.

How Training in Science Has Changed

In the past, the majority of newly trained scientists entered the ranks of university faculty. But the possibility of a career in industry has changed the way in which young scientists construe their career options. Realizing that fewer jobs are available in academia, many young scientists now consider a career in industry. In preparing for their future careers as scientists, students at all levels—high school, college, and graduate school—aim to acquire a strong background in business and management. Even if they decide to stay in academia, graduates with such training believe they will have a competitive edge over those who have spent most of their time exclusively in the lab.

Competition for professional positions in both industry and academia has spurred other shifts in training. Most relevant to the students we interviewed have been the "field changes" in the age at which individuals begin their "formal" training for a career in science. Because professional positions have become scarce,[2] some young people intent on becoming scientists begin preparing their résumés as early as high school. They seek positions in laboratories to gain first-hand research experience in academic settings and to get the opportunity to publish. Since most high schools do not offer high-level science courses, such laboratory positions connect students to local universities and research institutions. High school students working toward a career in science also participate in national and international science fairs, such as the Intel Science Talent Search (formerly underwritten by Westinghouse). If students achieve the rank of finalist or semifinalist in these competitions, this distinction often results in a lucrative scholarship and may constitute their first step in becoming known and connected in the field.

Students realize that in order to be a strong candidate for graduate admission, they must attend a "top" university. As undergraduates, most young geneticists major in biology and take courses in organic chemistry and genetics. They also work (in many cases, continue to work) in laboratories to gain research experience. Such an apprenticeship, they hope, will enable them to network with prestigious professors who can provide recommendations for admission to graduate school and help them to publish their work.

Not only does training start earlier now than it did in the past, but the time it takes to be "fully" prepared for a career in science has also increased. These days, earning a doctorate in science is standard. Interestingly, prior to the twentieth century, world-class scientists such as Michael Faraday and Charles Darwin rarely had college degrees, much less doctoral training. Even by the mid-twentieth century, only about half of the notable scientists in the United States had attended university.[3] Yet the 6,021 individuals who entered graduate programs in biomedicine in 1996 (compared to 1,887 in 1963) could expect to spend six or more years in graduate school.[4] Indeed, the average time students take to earn a doctorate has risen from 6.0 years in 1970 to 8.0 years in 1995.[5]

Though studies of inheritance began in the late nineteenth century, the creation of departments of genetics is a much more recent development. Currently, the graduate experience for fledgling geneticists consists of two phases: one to two years of coursework (typically, a student takes a total of six or seven courses), and a doctoral dissertation based on original research. While taking courses, students begin to work in a laboratory on a research project directed by a faculty member, and this research often becomes the focus of their dissertation. The arrangement is convenient for the students, who gain research experience and receive a stipend, and also for the principal investigators, whose research ideas and hypotheses are furthered by eager students willing to work hard to come up with publishable findings. It is in a professor's best interest to secure funding for his or her students; it is beneficial as well for the university, which receives outside funding (including overhead) and becomes known for innovative work.[6]

Even after this long period of training—so different from that of journalists—many young scientists decide to apply for postdoctoral study rather than seek a professional position. Postdoctoral fellowships have been called the "proving ground for academic excellence, scientific entrepreneurship, and ultimate intellectual independence."[7] They give budding scientists a chance to continue their research in a laboratory setting, publish their findings, and earn a modest income. Given the competition for jobs these days, it is not surprising that individuals are spending ever longer periods as postdoctoral fellows. Compared to scientists who were trained in the 1960s, many of whom spent only one or two years in postdoctoral programs, young scientists are now spending up to six years in such positions.

These long pre-career trajectories—sometimes dubbed "holding patterns"—have affected young scientists. Postdoctoral fellows, often in their late thirties, feel that they should be compensated fairly for their work, receive more benefits, and enjoy more flexible work conditions. As they search for their first "real job," many are torn between the higher salaries in the corporate world and the greater autonomy in the academy. Academic scientists have more independence in their work than their peers in biotechs, in terms of choosing both their topics and their methods. But they depend on grant money to support their research, and grant-seeking is anything but easy. Indeed, it is tremendously time-consuming and discouraging (most applications are turned down the first time), and the priorities of funding agencies do not always align with the interests of young scientists.

Who Are the Veteran Geneticists?

In our study of veteran professionals, we spoke primarily with individuals who had begun their careers in the 1960s and 1970s, when the domain of genetics was coming to the fore in dramatic fashion. Our participants were fortunate to have many choices; they could participate in academia or industry, or have a foot in both camps. Imaginative thinking and experimentation were encouraged, as the book on "the nature of life" was being rewritten on a yearly basis. While the pace of scientific discovery continues to be daunting, most young scientists entering the domain of science today are not so fortunate in the work conditions and options available to them.

From the beginning of our study in genetics, we recognized that different constituencies of scientists might have various perspectives on the domain and on their work in particular. We interviewed fifty-six professional geneticists, including Ph.D. researchers, M.D. researchers, industry-based researchers (biotech company founders and employees), and clinicians (genetic therapists who explain genetic risks to patients). Most of our participants were creators and leaders: they had made major discoveries in the field and often supervised important laboratories (for further details on the study of veterans, see the Appendix on Methods.)

The scientists with whom we spoke shared common domain values about the importance of science, the magnitude of its contributions to society, the need for open and unfettered exploration, and the imperative for scrupulous experimentation and precise reporting. While they were excited by the possibilities that emerged from their hard work, most of the veteran geneticists acknowledged the existence of ethical, social, and political issues. But they did not always agree on how to handle—or even who should handle—these issues.

Despite the rapid changes in the field, the veteran geneticists said they still believed in doing science "the old-fashioned way." Like journalists, these seasoned scientists most frequently mentioned integrity—honesty and thoroughness in procedures and reporting—as a standard critical for their own work and fundamental to the domain. Beatrice Mintz of the Fox Chase Cancer Center stated, "I can't imagine that anybody would be a scientist without believing in the importance of truth and integrity." Echoing the seasoned journalists, the older geneticists listed "Honesty and Integrity" as their most important professional value. Veteran participants also emphasized the excitement they found in scientific inquiry and in the open-minded exploration that is crucial to the scientific endeavor. A professor at Stanford University's School of Medicine spoke of his passion for discovery: it is, he said, "its own sort of addiction, or this high that you get when you actually discover something or do something that nobody's ever done before, or even overturn something that everybody held, . . . and you find out that all of that is bunk, and you have a whole new vision of what's correct."

Staying true to the principles of science was not the only goal of their work, however. Most of the scientists described careful and attentive work as a means to an important end: serving others. Nearly all of our veteran participants expressed a responsibility to society at large: two-thirds stressed the importance of keeping society informed and educated about scientific endeavors, nearly one-half mentioned helping people in general through their work, and one-quarter spoke of the need to minimize harm. Leroy Hood, at that time chair of the University of Washington's Department of Molecular Biotechnology, remarked: "A fundamental part of the scientist's obligation should be to communicate with society what science is about. And that's for a lot of reasons. One, you'd like to attract more good people into science. But even more important, you'd like to educate citizens so they can think about issues of science priority, science regulation, the ethical dimensions, and things like that."

Our exploration of responsibilities yielded one unexpected finding. While the scientists we interviewed were alert to the possibility that discoveries could be misinterpreted or misunderstood by the general public, more than half of them said that *other* individuals, such as people in government or members of the public, were responsible for determining the appropriate uses of scientific work. In our terms, these participants *imputed* responsibilities to others, rather than to themselves or their close colleagues. Paradoxically, however, most of these scientists admitted they did not have the time to educate policymakers or members of the public. So the situation was troubling: most of the scientists did not want to take responsibility for the implications of their work, yet they were unwilling to make a commitment to educate those to whom they imputed that responsibility.

It is important to note that these issues of application represent a recent trend. When these scientists began their careers thirty or forty years ago, research for product development was not common. But nearly 80 percent of those with whom we spoke in the late 1990s cited goals concerned with identifying diseases and cures and developing pharmaceuticals. A professor at the University of California at Berkeley remarked on this shift:

> You know, I started off, when I was a young scientist, a student, completely driven by just wanting to know, to dig out

the truth. And that's still the main driving force. But there's now a secondary fringe benefit. And that is that the body of work that we've done in the last thirty years or so can actually be applied in some very powerful ways. For new drug therapies, or understanding ways to treat disease. . . . I would say in the last ten years it's become much more interesting for me to also look at that other piece of biology, which is: How do I use my basic information in a way that could revolutionize drug discovery or disease?

Though they were excited by their work and by the opportunity to help humanity, the veteran geneticists spoke at length about the obstacles they faced: difficulties in finding time for a personal life, pressures to report results quickly, the need to deal with vexed ethical and legal implications of their work. One highly respected scientist speculated that she spent a third of the academic year (three months) writing standard proposals to the government and seeking alternative funding (money that would support nontraditional work—for example, involving application of findings or exploring more speculative paths). "The major amount of your time in the research is raising money," she explained. "That means day and night. Writing grants, writing renewals. And then also you have to of course pay your dues. . . . As soon as you get a grant, they say, 'Will you serve on a study section?' Then suddenly come sixty grants. So there's all these obligations in order to keep the engine going. Nobody really has a big enough endowment to just run a lab."

Academic scientists are often challenged with funding limitations even after they receive grant money. These scientists do not have the liberty (or the resources) to use funds to develop applications. The only way to secure funds for the production of a drug is to find a company to pay for it—a major reason many scientists have left university labs to pursue research in pharmaceutical companies. A professor at Princeton University described the dilemma of "going to a company where the issue of being in the world of health and being in the world of business was a balancing act and a conflict situation of very considerable proportions." Another scientist talked at length about the "social conscience" of the firm he worked for—a pharmaceutical company that developed drugs for HIV-positive patients "at all costs." He explained the significance of this decision: only a small percentage of the population infected with HIV would be able to afford the drug. Yet he also noted that the same company declined to produce a malaria vaccine. The reason was clear, and purely financial: few people in the United States would need malaria immunizations. As he pointed out, "Practical financial issues enter the decision process."

Many of the academic scientists in our study were worried about the future of university-sponsored research and expressed concern for individuals just entering the field. The veteran scientists wanted to encourage postdoctoral fellows to stay in academic laboratories (though there were fewer academic positions than industry jobs available), since this was where they thought vital basic research would continue to be done. They recognized the importance of serving as mentors for these young professionals—of showing how to handle the pressures and how to identify and seize exciting opportunities. Yet they knew that when graduate students and postdocs were faced with deciding between industry and academia, the opportunity for securing higher salaries and working on potentially dramatic applications could be quite seductive.

In sharp contrast to the "orphan" situation we identified in journalism, most of the veteran geneticists supervised younger teams of researchers and often described themselves as mentors. A scientist's mentor relationship with postdoctoral fellows, though sometimes competitive and even contentious, constitutes an important aspect of training. Well over half of the veteran participants said they felt a responsibility to their students and employees. They talked about assisting them in getting higher salaries, increasing their recognition, providing opportunities for authorship, and locating permanent positions. More than a third of the veteran geneticists—compared to a tiny minority of experienced journalists and veterans in theater—cited "Teaching and Mentoring" as a most important value for them personally. A professor at the University of Washington's Division of Medical Genetics characterized her mentoring responsibilities as similar to those of a parent:

> Those of us who have been in the field for quite a while have enormous respect and affection for the young people coming along. That it's parental in the very best sense. That you really feel a responsibility to help them along. You also feel, because it's absolutely essential, you've got to rely on them. They are the ones doing the work. You have to rely on their data. Your expectations of them are very high . . . and they have a right to expect absolute total loyalty from you. . . . That's another sort of value we share, which is the importance of the next academic generation.

Veteran geneticists spoke of their responsibilities to carry out high-quality work in a scientifically appropriate manner, and to model this behavior overtly for the younger professionals. The veterans cited mentoring as a motivating reason to stay in a university setting: they enjoyed providing guidance on how to handle challenges, such as the push to publish versus the need for experimental replication, or how to remain on good terms with competitors while advancing one's own career. Recognizing the fierce, competitive nature of individuals in their field, mentors tried to distance their students from the misbehavior that sometimes occurred. A professor who worked at Massachusetts Institute of Technology's Whitehead Institute remarked: "There are just a whole lot of people in science who use people. And I try very hard—and I don't always succeed, but I try hard—and actually do good by the people I have working for me." Such mentors publicly give credit to their mentees when it is due (as opposed to "scooping" or "stealing" data). Joan Steitz, professor of Molecular Biophysics and Biochemistry at Yale University, articulated this obligation:

> Well, one certainly needs to transmit excitement and curiosity. On the other hand, it's very important to transmit . . . standards of excellence: how you go about interfacing with your colleagues in terms of scientific integrity, in terms of making sure that the people who really did come up with the ideas and do the work are the people that get credit for it; and that there are certain very important standards as to how you actually behave in the field.

Another scientist said she not only gave appropriate credit to each individual by name, but also included the student's photograph when possible. "In creative work or scientific research where ideas really count, . . . it's the good ideas that count, that change people's minds. . . . It's very important to give credit all the time, to recognize that."

The veteran geneticists were most worried about the consequences of competitiveness in their field. Market pressures have led to hasty, less careful work and a reluctance to share information openly and honestly. The veterans struggled to find ways to warn students of their concerns. David Ledbetter, chair of the Department of Human Genetics at the University of Chicago, pondered this dilemma:

> So, to what degree should your discussions with young people be realistic versus idealistic? And I think most of my colleagues are extremely idealistic, and I don't know how much

of it is because they want to recruit students into their labs, so they don't want to say anything that might discourage them. . . . When they get a graduate student in their lab who's having a lot of difficulties, most people's response is to do everything possible to help them successfully complete the program, and it's very rare for them to say, "Well, let's re-evaluate whether you should be here." Which I think is the discussion that should come up early. Because it's better to be disappointed and change plans early rather than late.

Other scientists emphasized the importance of assuring students they would have the opportunity to work on interesting projects. One scientist said she went out of her way to secure enough funding so that she did not have to disappoint a student:

The point is to make it secure for young people to work on ideas that are really far out but important. You have to have sources of funding, so that when they write a grant and it gets turned down—which it always does if it's really new, it's the rule rather than the exception—they don't get depressed and give up. You have to say, "I've got another grant; we're going to 'bleed' off that for a little while. You just keep working and I'll worry about it."

The veteran professionals—who saw themselves as guiding, direct-ing, and mentoring a new generation—held strong values about how to engage in scientific work, how to relate and communicate with peers, and how to train students and postdoctoral fellows. Some of them also felt responsible for the consequences of their work—for ex-ample, that the mission of the domain of science be maintained and not abused. And some of them felt an obligation to communicate this value to the next generation. But as we have seen, the young scientists faced different kinds of struggles. They had to deal with a different kind of competition. For many budding geneticists, the bottom line may not entail receiving credit for a new scientific discovery; rather, it may involve securing a lucrative position with a firm that engages in secretive lines of research. Genetics has been called "the field of the future." But what kind of future lies ahead for these promising young geneticists?

Who Are the Young Scientists?

We interviewed thirty-three young scientists, mainly geneticists, at three levels: high school, graduate school, and the first few years of professional work (including postdoctoral research). Our sample included twelve high school students, eleven graduate students, five academic postdoctoral fellows, and five industry scientists. Of the high school students, almost half were first-generation Americans. Perhaps the potential to earn a lucrative salary had attracted these talented newcomers, yielding a more diverse group than our sample of young journalists (for further details, see the Appendix on Methods). Though we were focusing on geneticists—and the veterans and young professionals clearly fell into this category—few of the high school students had made a career commitment with that degree of specificity. So it would be better to think of the younger students as biological scientists. Accordingly, in the following discussion we generally use the term "scientist" rather than "geneticist."

Though the field has changed dramatically since the 1960s, the young scientists described familiar influences, experiences, and personal traits that shaped their entry into science. Like their predecessors in earlier eras, these individuals said they felt a "natural" inclination to science and mathematics starting in elementary school—a curiosity about causes and processes, a penchant for logic, and skill in manipulating small objects.[8] A seventeen-year-old high school student recalled, "I was always interested in why the dog was barking. Or why the rabbit's nose twitched that way and his ears went the other way." Many of these individuals reminisced about collecting bugs, climbing trees, observing nature. They spoke of observing crayfish in the fourth grade, and, in the sixth grade, competing in solar-car races that piqued their desire to persevere in this area of work. School-sponsored, hands-on research projects were also commonly cited as an important source of early interest in science.

Sometimes this early interest in science was nourished by parents, who gave carefully selected presents (microscopes, lab kits) or set an example as teachers and researchers in the field. A student at Lexington High School (in Lexington, Mass.) who was engaged in water pollution research described how his mother, a medical researcher, influenced his thinking as a young child: "My mom used to just point out how looking at something logically is much more useful than looking at it from a kind of abstract perspective, because you can learn more about it if you try and look at it objectively." Young scientists also said that visits to the laboratories of their parents or older siblings were pivotal moments in their childhood: they thought that working with the instruments was "neat" and something they wanted to pursue. Once in high school, they often signed up for more than the required number of science classes, and many also worked in laboratories outside of school. These students described daily routines that often included six hours at school and five hours at the lab.

Many students were on the alert for a project that they could enter in the highly respected Intel Science Talent Search. As the competition went into high gear, they were driven by the opportunity to win—to be recognized nationally and internationally as top student scientists (which would embellish their college applications) and to receive prize money. A seventeen-year-old high school scientist, who was participating in research at the Memorial Sloan-Kettering Cancer Center in New York City, knew from the time she was six years old that she wanted to enter the Intel competition: "I remember sitting down with my parents and watching [a competition], and I thought, 'Oh my God, that's so interesting.' And that kids that looked so young were able to understand a concept so complex. And somehow I felt that it was something I really wanted to do, and so I challenged myself, because I have always been that sort of person—to want . . . bigger and higher challenges."

Other students acknowledged the lure of financial gain from these competitions. A summer intern at the Dana Farber Cancer Institute remarked that, at first, her main goal for completing a research project in order to enter Intel had been to "get an idea of what research was like." But once she had achieved this aim, her second involvement in the competition centered on "how much money I could make, and then I kind of got greedy."

For many of the high school scientists, participating in the Intel Science Talent Search was a pivotal event. Unlike their peers in journalism, who worked in protected school settings, these high school scientists quickly faced the realities of the domain: peer competition, constraints and limitations on the type of work that could be done, inconsistent standards (manifested in the judging), and the risk of failure after many months of work. Toiling daily in university labs, they also witnessed the struggles of graduate students and postdoctoral fellows—their efforts to balance their personal and professional lives, maintain relationships with advisors and peers in other labs, and find ways to share data effectively and prudently.

Like the young journalists, these fledgling scientists were strongly committed to honesty and accuracy in their work. Many of them felt it was important to avoid "cutting corners" anywhere, because science was a "search for truth." In the inventory of values, the high school students ranked "Honesty and Integrity," "Search for Knowledge," "Quality of Work," and "Intrinsic Motivation / Enjoyment of the Activity" as most important to them. The budding professionals likewise favored three of these values, but selected "Creativity/Pioneering" over "Intrinsic Motivation/Enjoyment of the Activity." By the time their career was launched, young scientists were willing to sacrifice a certain degree of "flow"—a satisfying and all-encompassing involvement—in favor of pursuing ideas that were likely to earn them publications and tenure.[9]

Some of the young scientists described themselves as perfectionists, a trait they considered necessary for a skilled scientist. An eighteen-year-old high school student said, "You either make it perfect, or you don't do it at all." She used a phrase that epitomized the perfectionism apparent throughout the young professionals' discussions of their committed and devoted approach to science: "staying until the job is done." She also said she would never let anyone else in the lab record results for her, even if she had to make an extra trip just for this purpose. She trusted the data only if she recorded them herself.

Young professional scientists also described themselves as self-motivators and self-initiators. High school students spoke of finding placements in university labs on their own; they articulated the importance of developing an understanding of scientific procedures and concepts, without the need to rely on teachers or lab advisors and mentors. These students said they went to the library in their spare time and taught themselves material that had not yet been covered in class. Interestingly, a few of them did not want to reveal their age to the postdoctoral fellows in their lab, fearing they would lose credibility because they were so young.

At the same time, however, some of these students were still "just kids," as was obvious when they told us about the times they acted immaturely with their friends. Accounts of pranks, thefts, and dishonesty contrasted sharply with the sophisticated and professional demeanor of young scientists in the laboratory. A seventeen-year-old high school student expressed anger with a peer who copied data for her Intel project and did not appropriately credit the source, yet also told us that he had stolen collectible license plates from cars for "fun." Another high school student stole a banner from one of her school's sports teams. Though some may view these incidents as typical adolescent pranks, we were surprised to hear such tales from these students, who were in many ways mature "beyond their years" and preparing to enter the professional world. In fact, one of the high school scientists with whom we spoke, an intern in a laboratory at the Harvard Medical School, said she was frustrated with adults who stereotyped adolescents as "just kids," since many teenagers, such as herself and her science-oriented peers, were more advanced:

> When I first tried to look for a place to work, . . . I hit so many roadblocks. . . . Sometimes when people look at your age they expect something, or they have a stereotype of teenagers, and sometimes that's really what you don't want. . . . When I interned at that job [at a laboratory], they were surprised because we would have lunch together at lunchtime. And they'd be like, "Wow, I can actually talk to you and have a good conversation." And I was like, "Why would you not be able to? I don't understand why you'd ever think I couldn't hold a conversation."

A few young scientists mentioned personal hardships they had experienced growing up, such as losing a parent at an early age or living with a terminally ill grandparent. These family experiences led to their interest in medicine; budding physicians and scientists hoped to find a cure for a disease or develop an effective drug. One high school student talked of losing her father to cancer, saying, "That was one of the reasons why I pursued this research" (on melanoma and genetics). Though she had started out in science for the sake of her father, who wanted her to be a doctor, she had eventually formed her own goals. "My choice to become a doctor is not [to] satiate my father's dreams, but rather [to] satiate my own personal goal of trying to reach out to other people. And satisfy my need—my interest in science, as well as that need to reach out to other people."

Not only did several parents "jump start" their children's early interest in science; they also helped them to form values, beliefs, and approaches to work. In marked contrast to most of the young journalists and actors, the scientists typically said that their parents' backgrounds—their religion, ethnicity, and professional experiences—served as motivators and models. Several of the recent immigrants spoke admiringly of their parents' courage: of the challenges they had faced in coming to a new country and the difficulties they had encountered in adapting to new careers and new ways of life. A seventeen-year-old student of Russian extraction, a researcher at the SUNY Health Science Center at Brooklyn, explained how his parents' cultural and ethnic background and their integrity as professional exemplars had led him to science:

I come from a more science-type of family. My dad is a structural engineer. My mother is a nurse. So I have more of a science background. My dad also, he comes from the Soviet Union and . . . I don't think that the Soviets were such free thinkers. . . . They weren't allowed to express themselves so much, so they became great mathematicians, great physicists, and . . . they didn't really write so much. I mean, they read like Dostoevsky, or they read Tolstoy . . . but they don't really write their own stuff so much. They have to conform to society's standards. So . . . I guess I was more geared to thinking scientifically rather than . . . the way a humanities person would.

An eighteen-year-old student at Stuyvesant High School in New York City, a recent immigrant from Syria, talked of the pressure from his parents, who had come to the United States in order to give their children career opportunities:

> I came here, and my parents came here and they constantly remind me that they came here, so that I could have more opportunity. They worked really, really hard to get me through school. To save up enough money so we could go to college. They always tell me that this is just for me. So that I can have all the opportunities I want. So that I can do whatever I want. Although they also tell me I have to be a doctor. . . . I felt that their coming here was for me. I want their coming here to have been useful, and them not to regret it. I keep being reminded of that because every time I am successful in something, getting into my high school, getting into college, my parents say it's things like this that keep them from regretting leaving their country.

A burning desire to earn money and live comfortably was notable in the testimony of these high school students. Their aspirations differed from the hopes identified by the other young professionals with whom we spoke, and probably also from the goals that budding scientists pursued several decades ago. A third of the high school students (mostly males) ranked "Wealth and Material Well-Being" as one of the four most important values to them personally (as opposed to professionally). None of the young professionals or the veteran professionals identified this value as most important. At Midwood High School in Brooklyn, New York, a public high school known for producing Intel winners, students talked about becoming "starving scientists" the way one might speak of "starving artists."[10] Consider what we heard from a senior at a prestigious high school science academy:

> My reasoning is kind of funny in this part, because when I was a little bit younger, like a few years younger, I totally wanted to be a research scientist. I wanted to go into the Center for Disease Control and do research with the diseases and do that type of stuff. But as I grew older, I began to need a lot of money, and I began to see people's nice cars and things like that. . . . So that's why I considered it—because as I grew up, I began to see the need for money and what you can do with it. And I guess being a doctor and not a research scientist, you make a little more money that way. And you get satisfaction from helping people out. So I think I'm leaning towards being a doctor, mostly because of financial reasons.

A handful of individuals said they were attracted to science because of their religious beliefs. They saw scientific research as a spiritual pursuit—a way of getting close to God, of fulfilling a purpose in life which had been determined by a higher power. This sentiment was not expressed by any of the young journalists. A seventeen-year-old student at Townsend Harris High School in New York explained that as a Guyanese Indian "I believe that everybody has a time and place to live. And that we're all connected in some way, shape, or form. I believe that everybody has a purpose in life, and once that purpose is fulfilled they will pass away. . . . I am not sure what my mark is, but I'm hoping that I'm going along the right way in pursuing . . . research, and going this way I will be fulfilling that purpose." A young Asian American woman felt that God was guiding her in her work: "I go to church and I believe in God. And I believe that you're here to do the right thing. I mean, trying to get around things and stuff—that's not the way you're supposed to be. You're here to do the right thing. And if you can do that, then that's [the] job." A fifth-year postdoctoral fellow at Harvard University, age thirty-four, saw science and religion as inextricably linked: "I think about how nature works as being so mysterious. And understanding that on a spiritual level—understanding how the world works or how the universe is organized—that's as close to God as you can get. To put it in religious or spiritual terms, that's what I would say science is. As close to God as you can get is to try to understand as deeply as you can something about the world or about life."

Despite such personal testimonials, only two young professionals ranked "Religion" or "Spirituality" as a relatively important aspect in their professional lives. Several young scientists articulated the value of religion during the interviews. Yet when asked to rank a list of values in order of importance, these individuals selected other values, such as "Accuracy" and "Integrity," as more important for their work.

In addition to family background, supportive teachers were often mentioned by young scientists. These mentors recommended participation in school science fairs and helped students prepare for such "friendly" competitions. Students at all levels searched for "good advisors" who would show them how to approach research design, how to deal with peers and colleagues, and how and when to publish findings. They looked for clues about personal issues, such as the best way to achieve balance in their lives. And many graduate students and postdoctoral fellows hoped that their advisor would recommend them for their next position, whether in an academic or industrial setting; accordingly, they approached this relationship with considerable care. Echoing the testimony of the veteran scientists, young scientists reported that these professionals took their mentoring role seriously;

they strove to set an example by performing work that was high quality and principled.

When asked to rank values in order of preference, young scientists concurred with veteran geneticists on the importance of "Teaching and Mentoring." This was not always the case for young professionals in other domains; in theater, for example, directors were not necessarily viewed by their students as individuals having a vested interest in those who worked for them. Young actors often cited "director abuse" as one of the most difficult pressures in their work. On occasion, young scientists did report situations in which they felt misguided. A graduate student at the Massachusetts Institute of Technology noted that being a mentor is not always natural or easy: "People who become advisors are selected because they are great scientists, not because they are managers or because they have well-developed interpersonal skills. So you get these people who have spent their whole life at a bench, and all of a sudden they're in charge of fifteen people. Where were they supposed to learn?"

Integrity, Competition, and Survival

Teachers, advisors, and mentors have a challenging role to play in guiding young professional scientists. Throughout their training, young scientists today encounter situations that challenge their rigorous scientific approaches, their personal and professional values of honesty and integrity, and their sense of responsibility to the wider world. In what follows we describe three different kinds of dilemmas that young professionals in our study regularly faced. In each of the scenarios, an individual had to determine how to remain true to his or her professional standards, goals, and ambitions, while simultaneously achieving what he or she had spent long years preparing for (whether an Intel placement that entailed scholarship money, or an attractive professional position).

Costs and Rewards (Living with Authority)

Mark, thirty years old, was in his fifth year of graduate study in a department of genetics where he was working toward a Ph.D. in molecular biology. He liked to refer to himself as an applied scientist, since he always asked the question, "What's the human value?" His long-standing stated goal was to help human beings.

Mark confronted a situation in which his instinctive altruism came into conflict with his ambition to become a recognized professional. Unless he was willing to be "scooped," he had to consider carefully whether to share new work with colleagues. He was working concurrently on two projects. The first aimed at curbing a potentially fatal human disorder by developing an animal model that could ultimately lead to better treatments and diagnostic measures. The second—a project that Mark had dubbed his "soapbox"—was situated in the emerging field of computational biology. Its goal was to develop a tool that would allow molecular biologists to sift through the abundant data generated by the human genome project. Mark wanted to ensure that scientists could use and share available data. "There's all this awesome, great data out there that we can use," he said. "Let's just figure out how to use it."

One facet of this project was the investigation of national and international databases. Mark learned of an organization that was producing flawed data, and subsequently tried to discourage the spread of these data by contacting higher-ups at the organization. After many letters and no responses, he finally contacted the "second in command" at a prestigious institution. He sent this individual a statement of his objections concerning the faulty data source, and to support his argument further he included his own unpublished data.

The person with whom Mark finally connected was extremely appreciative. Mark was hopeful that the institution would henceforth be more careful about how and from whom they accepted data: "They've eliminated certain companies that have given them error-prone data before. They're not accepting anything from them anymore. They've installed systematic evaluations, like we suggested."

But a few weeks later, his contact at the institution (whom he described as his "friend" because of the relationship they had developed) posted Mark's data set on a website without asking permission and without giving proper credit. Perplexed, Mark approached representatives of the institution. One representative "admitted that we were the driving force to changing the way the database is going, but he gave some excuses and he did whatever and then that was it." When Mark approached professors in his home institution for help, "they said, 'This is the way it happens. This is science politics.'"

The incident disappointed Mark for several reasons. First, he did not receive appropriate credit for his work. Second, there seemed to be nothing that he could do about it, since the person who had stolen his data and neglected to give him credit was in a higher position of authority—he had the power to ruin Mark's career. Many professors, including Mark's mentor, counseled him not to write a letter of complaint. They all advised against doing anything that would hurt his chances of getting a recommendation from the person: "[This] is ten times more important for you—getting a recommendation from this guy—than not having him as a friend." Third and most important, the incident made Mark realize that his scientific values and beliefs were not aligned with those of most of his colleagues:

> It's affected the way I think about the field. Because I used to
> think it was all holy up there. . . . [I] used to think, "Okay,
> scientists go into this as these intellectual people trying to

solve the problems of our society." And they're not flashy. You look at us, we're all wearing T-shirts, whatever. We're not trying to impress anybody like that, but we're just trying to think. And then I see . . . the same sort of low-life interaction you see on all these other levels, and it just brings down my image of the field.

Mark was grateful to his mentor for showing him how to navigate the "real life" of science politics. He described his mentor as almost a "big brother" who "kept telling you at every stage whether you had a problem . . . [or] whether [this was] reality." But the personal goals and ethical orientations that Mark had grown up with were forever tainted. "Every time I make [a] judgment . . . I'll think twice. I mean, it sounds bad, but I'll think twice about doing that if I stay in the field. I'm not saying that I still won't, but I'll definitely think twice. Maybe I'll write it a different way, maybe I'll give him limited information. But I'll definitely think twice about how I do it. Which is sad. . . . I'm haunted by those decisions and the outcomes of those decisions."

In the end, Mark decided that if he remained in the field, he was going to have to play "hardball": "I don't understand it. I'm not sure I agree with it. But if I'm going to stay in this field, that's the way. You've got to abide by these rules." Mark decided that he was not always going to make the application and utility of his work a priority. He was going to have to find a way to balance his ultimate goal of making his work beneficial and helpful to others with the need to protect himself as a young professional in the field. He realized that his values and morals would be "separated from what happens in science." In his own "last" words: "Screw the scientific value of it. Screw the success. I think that's really important . . . making both worlds work. You want to be able to survive in your field. Just be able to survive.

Just be able to live and make a living. At the same time, you need to do what's right. There will probably need to be a way that I could do both. Without getting screwed over."

Young professional scientists today must navigate their way in the face of fierce competition—which sometimes comes from those in positions of authority. Lab advisors are scrambling to secure the same governmental funds that their students hope to be granted. One postdoctoral fellow said that when she had applied for a position at a lab, her prospective employers had credited her advisor for the work she herself had carried out. Another postdoctoral fellow, at the Massachusetts Institute of Technology, commented that dealing with an advisor is both similar to and different from a parent-child relationship: "It's like parenting kids, in many senses. The kids feel ready to be independent long before the parent has decided that they are. So you go through this rebellion phase. But unfortunately we're all disguised in this professional environment, so you can't spike your hair and scream, 'I hate you!' You have to do something else, like say, 'Well, I disagree with your hypothesis.'"

Beyond question, the young scientists at all levels had a code of ethics for their work: they spoke spontaneously and repeatedly of honesty, accuracy, and objectivity as natural and imperative standards. But many fledgling professionals like Mark confronted situations in which they were forced to choose among competing loyalties, especially when their future careers appeared to be at stake. Although some young professionals considered changing the ways they worked in the field in order to protect themselves, others talked about surrounding themselves with like-minded professionals in environments where they hoped they would be able to act in a responsible manner. Specifically, young professionals thought their situation might change if they had the opportunity to work for a different advisor, lab, or company. In other words, they hoped that it was their current workplace—a reflection of today's field—and not the domain of science per se, that was testing the durability of their personal values. In terms of our larger study, they were trying to create environments in which their own personal values were well aligned with those of the profession.

Yet it is not fair to assume that all of the young scientists were in danger of sacrificing their personal standards and values. We heard from some young professionals who managed to uphold their code of ethics despite such pressures. A graduate student at the Massachusetts Institute of Technology stood her ground despite pressure from her advisor and committee members. After she had obtained promising data from two of the three experiments she had set out to complete, her advisors wanted her to publish partial findings. One advisor maintained that "you just can't expect to make sense of everything. . . . Your experiments on these two that make sense are strong—and believe them, believe in yourself, go ahead, publish them." But she felt that the third experiment might produce data that would throw the overall argument into doubt. Ultimately, she said, "I decided it was unethical. . . . Much as it may be great for me to put it out there, . . . I don't want to take the risk." "All you have in science is your reputation," she reflected. "It was not worth my reputation, and it would slow progress in the field. . . . Especially when you're trying to put out something that you think is high quality." For some young professionals, establishing a reputation as someone who does good work is more important for building a career than the lure of short-term fame and fortune.

BEYOND THE SCIENCE CLUB (LIVING WITH OTHERS)

For the high school scientists, competition was also a reality, especially for those who took part in the Intel Science Talent Search. These high school students wanted *everything* that Intel had to offer: the recognition, the money, the elite status, the social networks, and the personal satisfaction. For many, the competition was fierce—so much was at stake—and the students' espoused standards of honesty and accuracy proved vulnerable. In the case of a high school senior named Allison, the drive to win ultimately eclipsed her scientific conscience.

Allison had always enjoyed science more than any other subject. At a prestigious "exam" high school, during the second semester of her sophomore year, she enrolled in a research program that connected students with local research institutions so that they could conduct a project for the Intel competitions. Allison was introduced to a well-known professor at a major university in New York City who immediately invited her to work in her neurobiology lab.

At their first meeting, the professor offered Allison a number of different projects on which she could work. This was an unusual and fortunate circumstance, since high school students were normally assigned to projects that needed an extra hand. Allison decided on her own to work on a learning experiment involving mice. This was not an easy choice, for two reasons: she did not like handling animals (especially mice); and more important, the professor warned her that projects based on neurology and behavior of "live" animals did not seem to capture the fancy of the Intel judges. This advice did not deter Allison, however; over the years, the Intel competitions had been characterized by inconsistent judging.

During the summer between her junior and senior years in high school, while working at the lab, Allison received additional training through scientific reading and writing workshops. Like many high school students, Allison had a hard time balancing her social life with her academic obligations and her commitment to her position in the lab. She often stayed up until two in the morning to finish her homework, and met her friends at the lab when she had a break. "It was hard work sometimes, but I think it was worth it," she said.

Allison maintained strong values about the ways in which scientists should work. She believed in honesty—in not fabricating data, not stealing data, and not taking credit for work that was not one's own. She was aware that nowadays not all scientists honor these norms. In her opinion, appropriate punishment would be "public humiliation. . . . I think that just goes against the way the scientific field should work, and I guess they'd be blacklisted if they worked like that." Allison also felt responsibility to the domain of science: the purpose of experiments was to build knowledge for the field. She talked about the importance of honest reporting: "If you lie in the course of an experiment, or if you take information from other scientists, the stuff that can happen—you really see the effects and it's hard to tell a little white lie when you're doing a big experiment, because you're affecting data."

But there was another side to Allison: her fierce desire to win a competition—for herself, for the personal recognition, and for the scholarship money. She enjoyed the competition inherent in Intel; she thought of it as an athletic event. She spoke admiringly of *The Double Helix,* a book that chronicles the intense competition for the discovery of the structure of DNA and suggests that scientific ends may justify ethically dubious means.

This tension between what Allison wanted (and felt she deserved) for herself and the standards she held for scientific work became palpable when she faced the decision about how to write her research paper for the Intel competition. Knowing that she was unlikely to win, because she had worked directly with animals, Allison decided to hide the truth. "I had to phrase my paper really particularly so it didn't look like I was actually touching the animals and stuff like that. I had to say that I had watched videos."

> I didn't think it was fair that I couldn't get rewarded for my work because I worked with animals. . . . That just made me mad, so I didn't care. . . . Maybe it was lying in a way, but I

didn't think that it was wrong, because I deserved to be rewarded. . . . I did the work—it wasn't that someone else did
it. It was my work, and I did record it. I did make videos and
stuff like that, but I thought that it was fair because I think
that I deserved the recognition that other people did that
worked just as hard if not less than I did.

In the end, Allison was named a semifinalist and won a college
scholarship worth $2,000. It is unclear whether her professor in the
lab or her teachers at school knew that she had withheld important information in her final research report. It is clear that, like some of our
errant journalists, she did not feel bad about what she had done, nor
did she feel that she should be "blacklisted" from the scientific community. In fact, Allison was accepted at an Ivy League university,
where she chose to pursue scientific research. Her professional goal
was to conduct research in molecular or cell biology and teach at the
graduate level.

Allison was by no means an isolated case. Several students told us that
in shaping their projects to win the Intel competitions, they were acting much like professional scientists who prepare grant applications
for foundation and governmental funding. They chose "safe" topics
that they knew would be of interest, and they submitted proposals
that were not written in a wholly truthful manner. Certainly, the Intel
competitions, which presented opportunities for a small cohort of students to earn substantial sums, contributed to the pressures to engage
in deceptive behavior. There will always be students who cheat to get
an A, the grade that will get them into the college of their choice.

It seems clear that even our high school students were well aware of
the tensions between their own high personal standards and their desire to be successful in society at large. They deplored their elders

whose behavior was marked by dishonesty. Yet what emerged in our study, time and again, was the willingness of some young people to compromise their values, or hold them in abeyance, in order to gain a temporary advantage on their way to professional success. We need to understand how young people come to value expediency over integrity and whether this evaluation can be reversed.

"Can I Afford to Be a Scientist?" (Living with Self)

Many of the young scientists commented that in these difficult times, it is imperative to maintain a balance between personal life and professional life. Some even mentioned switching fields so they would at least be able to maintain their personal lives along with a comfortable style of living. Sometimes, as happened with the high school scientists we interviewed, this dilemma led to a decision to spurn academic research. Though they all wanted to stay involved with science in some way, these young scientists were concerned about the lack of personal time, the fierce competition for a few choice spots, and uncertain financial stability.

Maria was a sixth-year graduate student in molecular biology, working in the lab of a well-known professor at a small university. As a child and adolescent she had played the violin, and had considered a career as a musician. But when deciding about college, she had chosen an academic route. Maria felt that her violin training had been helpful for her work in science: it had taught her endurance and discipline—both of which are requirements for a scientist. While an undergraduate studying microbiology, Maria had considered applying to medical school. Yet after some favorable experiences working in a lab, she had decided she wanted to pursue research. Working as a research assistant, Maria had started to network, a step she believed was key for securing a position in a lab that focused on how to repair broken chromosomes.

At the time we spoke with her, Maria was unsure about her ultimate career path. She was considering positions in both academic and industry settings. She had applied for a few jobs but was not confident about getting them, because of the heated competition.

> I'm in a particularly bad point because now I'm in the competition. Right now, applying for fellowships . . . it's not a good feeling. . . . And so it's a lot of pressure right now. I think one way or the other I'll be OK, but I just think, you know, you've just got to keep working. I've seen a lot of bad things happen to some people who I think really deserve to get positions, whether it's here or in other countries, and they haven't. And I just feel how horrible it is. And there's no reason to think it's not going to happen to me too.

Maria was also worried about earning a viable salary:

> The pressure I have now is real-life pressure. It's my life. I'm trying to get money to do this now. The pressure before is sort of this pseudo-pressure that they put on you. OK, I am tired—I'm thirty-one years old and I'm tired of not having money. I am getting to the point now where it's pretty annoying to live with roommates, and I'm really ready to have—you know, people my age have kids and a family, . . . go out to dinner a couple of times a week, and things like that. And I'm just always scraping for money. And I'm getting pretty sick of that.

Maria felt pressure not only to make money and maintain a satisfactory income, but also to "have some sort of family life." She believed that "it's just really hard to be a woman in science. . . . There's very few women who . . . have a family and children and then run a lab. . . . Doing full-time research and having children do not go

together. They do not mix. And most anyone would tell you that."
She worried that she might have to leave science in order to maintain some kind of balance between her personal life and professional career.

> If I could find something else, realistically find something
> else at this point that allowed me to be creative and every
> day do something that I enjoy doing, then that's fine. Like
> playing violin, for instance. . . . You cannot possibly [become a scientist] nowadays and be able to have kids. And
> I've seen it, and it [has] happened right next door to us. So a
> woman tried it, failed, she's leaving science, OK? . . . I do
> know I want to have a family. . . . I'm not quite sure how it's
> going to happen.

In contrast to Mark, who was dealing with an egotistical senior figure, and Allison, who was engaged in a contest with her peers, Maria faced internal tension between her professional ambitions and her personal needs. On the one hand, she wanted to be able to run a lab and publish the requisite papers; on the other, she also wanted to be able to afford a family, in terms of both time and money. If Maria's dilemma seems different from the ones faced by Mark or Allison, this is because it was internal to her own psyche, rather than a conflict that directly affected her relations with her superiors or colleagues in the workplace. Still, Maria's dilemma was an ethical one as well. On the one hand, she felt a responsibility to those who trained her, and to the domain of science as whole. Was it right for her to turn her back on all those institutions and individuals who had invested in her and also to allow her expertise to go unused? She felt a responsibility to those in her personal world. On the other hand, was it proper for her to devote herself totally to her professional work, especially at the expense of loved ones?

Scientists at various professional stages agreed that the value of "Rewarding and Supportive Relationships" was important. Moreover, the importance of this value increased steadily as individuals progressed to the next professional stage in their career. Presumably this trend occurred because the scientists found it more difficult to balance family and professional life as they became more committed to a career of experiments and fundraising. And it was more likely to be cited by young women scientists, who were wondering whether it was possible to have a career in science and at the same time start a family. Yet achieving a balanced life was a concern even for the young people in our study. A seventeen-year-old Intel finalist commented, "If you want to be the best in the field, and if you want to do the groundbreaking research, you have to go the extra mile. And there's always someone out there working harder. And if you want to lead a balanced life, then you're not going to be the best."

But what is "the best"? Is the best scientist the one who makes a discovery first? The director of a well-funded laboratory? A researcher who publishes articles while still in high school? Or is being the best about doing work that is accurate, honest, and objective—work that is helpful to others, not only to other scientists but also to the wider public?

Wrestling with Ethical Dilemmas

As with our young journalists, we undertook more targeted probes in two areas: the sense of responsibility felt by the young scientists, and their responses to a hypothetical ethical dilemma. Across all age groups, the young scientists expressed a clear sense of responsibility to society and to others. This finding is encouraging in light of the stereotype of the "cut-throat" competitiveness of professionals in this domain.

Remarkably, the young scientists we interviewed seemed to act on their sense of responsibility: they all did volunteer work. Many of them assisted younger students by tutoring them in mathematics or science, while others devoted time to nursing homes, soup kitchens, and local libraries. Two individuals started clubs: one student founded a club called "Save the Manatee," which aimed at increasing students' awareness of environmental issues, particularly the plight of the manatees in Florida. Another individual founded the "Renaissance Committee," an effort to recognize and reward students achieving in areas outside academics and athletics. Through these experiences, students came to empathize with those in need, an experience that might inspire them to continue service work in the future.[11] Though some of these students discussed the importance of religion in their lives, only one young scientist drew a link between her volunteer work and her religion or place of worship. In general, these young scientists did not cite religious motivation for their service.

Most of the young scientists mentioned responsibilities that were a blend of selfish and selfless motivations. Both the high school students and the young professionals spoke of a responsibility to earn a satisfactory income, maintain a balance between their professional lives and personal lives, and adhere to personal values such as truth, honesty, and accuracy. As these novices attempted to navigate successful entry into the domain, they had to take steps to advance their careers—for example, publish scientific papers and secure grant funding. We learned that they were often expected to sacrifice deeply held beliefs, and that some of them yielded to these pressures.

At both professional stages, a sizable majority of young scientists imputed responsibility to others. Young scientists sometimes imputed responsibility to individual senior scientists, but for the most part they placed the burden on society at large. For example, a graduate student conducting research on genetic factors in obesity remarked that the fate of potentially harmful applications of his work should be decided by the voting public and the legislators they elect. "Ethics and society get very mixed," he noted. "I definitely try not to get into the realm of asking the questions, 'What is this going to be used for? What are the societal implications?' Because that's not my job. My job is to do the science. It's [up to] somebody else to figure out." The high school scientists shared many of these sentiments, though they also felt that they were not old enough or experienced enough to take on many of the ethical issues they raised. Considering whether scientists have a responsibility for the kind of research that gets done, such as cloning, one eighteen-year-old high school scientist commented: "I can voice my opinion and try to convince people this is what I think. . . . But other than that, . . . I'm just a kid that's trying to get to college." Across the age groups, rarely if ever did the scientists raise the question—one that is integral to most religious and ethical traditions—of whether the responsibility *should* fall on them if no one else is willing to assume it.

When journalists identified issues that transcended the scope of their responsibilities, they largely imputed responsibility to others within the profession. Difficult day-to-day decisions were often said to be the province of editors and news directors. Responding to criticism from readers or viewers was seen as the job of ombudsmen. Critical consideration of larger issues in the field was assigned to domain gatekeeping institutions, such as the Project for Excellence in Journalism at the Columbia School of Journalism. Thus, even when responsibility was imputed to others, it was still viewed as the duty of those within the field of journalism. Indeed, the journalists seemed as leery of outside agencies as the scientists seemed on the lookout for them.

The scientists also differed from the journalists in their views of future responsibilities. Several young scientists said that they would inherit responsibilities once they were in a position of authority. The journalists, on the other hand, made few statements to indicate that in the future they would assume responsibility that they did not currently hold. This reflects the fact that relatively few journalists in the study planned to assume positions as editors or news directors—the individuals to whom they most often imputed responsibility. Instead, they hoped to continue in journalism as reporters or broadcast anchors. In contrast, many of the young scientists were training for leadership positions—teaching at universities and directing research laboratories.

The most notable difference in the responses of younger and older scientists was evident in their discussions of responsibility to the domain of science. Whereas only one-third of the high school scientists mentioned a responsibility to the domain of science, twice as many of the young professionals and veterans articulated a responsibility to the "mission" of the domain—its treasured standards and practices. The high school students often talked of loyalties to their teachers and lab advisors, those local figures who helped them with their work on a daily basis and whom they saw as their models.

As in the ethics survey for journalism, the scientists we interviewed were also given hypothetical dilemmas, in which they indicated and discussed levels of concern (ranging from no concern to great concern) about particular ethical and moral issues. The prompt that we used read as follows:

> Suppose a scientist of your acquaintance discovered the gene for a monogenic disease from publicly funded research. Which of the following would raise an ethical issue or would be cause for moral concern, and why?
>
> 1. Withholding information relating to the gene from the scientific community and public until the gene is patented

2. Patenting the gene

3. Licensing the patent for profit to a pharmaceutical company or starting one's own company based on the discovery

4. Developing a genetic screen to detect susceptibility to getting the disease, and sharing the results with the patient's family, employer, and/or provider of health insurance

5. Creating categories of "genetic acceptability" among workers and job applicants, even if carriers of the disease are predominantly from ethnic or minority groups

6. Amniocentesis and genetic counseling of pregnant women or couples informing them of the likelihood of having offspring with the disease, and sharing (in some cases encouraging) options to divert such a possibility, including sterilization and abortion

7. Developing gene therapy to counteract effects of the defective gene in somatic tissue

8. Germ-line gene therapy

9. Large-scale genetic engineering on human populations for purposes of eugenics or "genetic farming."

Not surprisingly, both groups expressed great concern about the most dramatic conditions listed, such as "large-scale genetic engineering." Yet for many of the controversial topics, neither the high school scientists nor the young geneticists displayed concern. Roughly half of respondents marked "no concern" for germ-line gene therapy, genetic counseling, and gene therapy for a defective gene. Across age levels, most scientists felt that with the exception of "genetic engineering," if the possibilities could be used for something helpful, such as curing a patient with cancer, and if they were not abused (for example, by using cloning to produce a human being for organ farming), then there should be "no concern."

In discussing their level of concern, the young religious scientists used their faith in God to help determine "right from wrong." "I think your religious beliefs drive your morals," said one young scientist. "And your morals regulate how much you should do in science." She knew something was wrong when "you're trying to play God." A young member of the Eastern Orthodox branch of Catholicism likewise said that religion influenced her thinking on difficult issues like cloning. "I don't think anybody has a right to play God's role, you know? And that's what they're . . . doing. I don't like that. That's scary."

In comparison to the younger scientists, the veteran scientists generally expressed equivalent or greater concern regarding almost all of the issues on the survey. Interestingly, though, this trend was inverted on a single issue: financial profit. The possibility of "licensing a gene for profit" was of "great concern" to almost half of the high school respondents, whereas far fewer young professional geneticists and veteran professionals felt this was of "great concern." Of those high school students who marked "great concern," most were male.

As mentioned earlier, the high school students (particularly the young men) were concerned about the financial viability of a career in genetics. Financial insecurity was the main reason so many of these young individuals were not considering basic scientific research as a long-term career. At the same time that earning money was important to them, the idea that a scientist could make money from *publicly funded research* evoked moral concern on the part of the young scientists. They had drawn clear distinctions in their minds about the appropriate roles, responsibilities, and rewards of particular workplaces and fields within the domain of science.

We can say with confidence that the domain mission and standards for scientific work were well known even to the youngest scientists in our study. Moreover, with few exceptions, our participants respected those who practice these values and strove to emulate them. The difficulties they faced arose in two contexts. First, our participants sometimes felt they did not have sufficient power or authority to act on their values; they looked to others to pick up the challenge. When faced with situations about how to prioritize conflicting values or responsibilities, young scientists looked to their seniors for advice about how to make these decisions. Second, they were consumed by the daunting, daily tasks of finishing their training in order to become professionals, and had little time to spend struggling with the broad ethical issues that pervaded their work. Much like the young journalists, these young scientists seemed confident that once they had achieved professional success they would be able to return to their core values, which would be preserved untarnished, and to a more direct confrontation of ethical dilemmas.

Yet as in the domain of journalism, changes in technology and the pressures of the market clearly influenced the ways in which our participants worked in the field of science. The pace of scientific work has increased, competition has intensified, and the prospect of making money looms large. In our study, the impact of these changes was palpable: the young scientists were pressured to cut corners in their research and to publish data prematurely. If they did not keep up the pace, they feared being scooped—having their data reported before they could report it themselves. The young scientists were trying to uphold their beliefs and values about ethical work, while at the same time contributing new knowledge accurately and expeditiously to the scientific community and society at large.

For some young professionals, this challenge had become too difficult to manage. At the outset of their careers, some individuals like Maria were already considering leaving the profession. A graduate student who had spent six years training at the Massachusetts Institute of Technology said: "I'm really considering leaving, going and getting a job in business or law or anything that will take me, because although I really want to be a professor, I do not want to go through being a postdoc. The investment is so high that the fact that the possible payoff is so low is a real issue." Even some of the high school students, observing the stressful and insecure lives led by postdoctoral fellows, decided to follow a smoother career path.

Those young professionals who choose to stay in the field can expect to face many challenges: finding governmental funds and securing positions despite intense competition, staying true to scientific methods and principles in a fast-paced, technology-driven environment, and maintaining personal lives while spending long hours in the laboratory. They will certainly continue to confront situations in which they will be forced to prioritize their personal and professional responsibilities. These young professionals have spent many years planning and training to be top-flight experts, and no doubt some of them will make discoveries of genuine import. But will those who become leaders be prepared as well to resolve these internal struggles and to serve as tenable role models for a succeeding generation of scientists?

4

The Price of Passion in Theater

HOWEVER GLAMOROUS IT MAY APPEAR, the world of theater has always been rife with difficulties and surrounded by controversy. Actors have been considered vagabonds, prostitutes, and fools, and at times have even been denied burial rights accorded to other citizens.[1] Aspiring actors face fierce competition and constant rejection. The roles they do win are often separated from one another by extended periods of unemployment. They typically work long, irregular hours, travel frequently for work, and endure tedious memorizing of lines and repetitive rehearsals. Only the most talented gain regular employment, and very few achieve wide recognition and significant financial remuneration. Most actors struggle to survive in the profession and take what parts they can.[2] Even when their talent has been acknowledged, it is often dismissed as a matter of luck. And if they attain celebrity status, they are objectified by their audience and their privacy is violated by the media. Despite these many obstacles, the allure of theater continues to draw many aspirants.

In the United States there has long been an obsession with performers because they possess power, or at least a certain kind of influence. The most visible celebrities earn high salaries and epitomize glamour. We are drawn to actors because through their work they make private emotions public, guiding us through our world and other possible worlds. By watching emotions and events unfold on the stage or screen, we gain insights and deepen our understanding of ourselves.

At the same time, acting, especially on the stage, has long been a career that most parents—except, of course, the small but notorious group of "stage mothers"—do not wish for their children. This reluctance probably stems from the economic instability and social stigma associated with theater. The Puritans "were not only hostile to all pleasures but professed a special abhorrence for the stage,"[3] and this censorious view had a lasting impact on future generations. In the modern day much of that stigma is due to the influence of vaudeville, with its associations of loose women and unreliable men. But it is important to recall that "legitimate" theater, including serious drama or even comedies by Molière or Shakespeare, was also performed. Also contributing to the challenges of a life in theater is the fact that, historically, only a small sector of the performance community has wielded influence and commanded high pay, while the majority of actors have been less privileged.

Several shifts over the past century may have helped to establish theater as a legitimate profession in the United States. Perhaps most notable is the influence of the labor movement, especially the formation of the Actor's Equity Association in 1913.[4] Prior to the formation of the union, producers had set their own working conditions and pay scale, rehearsal time had been unregulated, and actors had received no compensation for rehearsals or holidays.[5] The Actors' Equity Association united individuals who were committed to working in theater as a profession rather than an avocation.[6] Professionalization of the domain was also fostered by the specialized theater schools that began to emerge at the end of the nineteenth century.[7] With the introduction of professional training programs, acting came to be recognized as a technique that could be studied and mastered. The renaissance of regional repertory theaters in the 1960s also broadened theater's venue across the United States.[8] Finally, the job security that came with studio contracts for actors working in film helped to ensure more regular paid employment, and did much to establish acting as a viable career.

Unlike genetics, where many years of formal training are virtually mandated, there is no obligatory regimen for the aspiring actor. Indeed, inborn talent, relentless effort, and keen collaborative skills may be as important as courses or diplomas. David Belasco, a prominent nineteenth-century playwright, director, and theater manager, asserted that for an actor's success, "the all-important essential is ability."[9] Twentieth-century actor and educator Uta Hagen concurs: "For a would-be actor, the prerequisite is *talent*. You can only hope to God you've got it."[10] But success in the profession depends equally on hard work, and as actor Simon Callow discovered early in his career, "actors were made not born."[11] Actors need all of the life and performance experience they can get. Also important are "character and ethics, a point of view about the world in which you live and an education."[12]

As noted repeatedly by our veteran informants, theater is collaborative in both effort and product. Ideally, it is a relationship among equals. Collaboration is not simply about compromise; maintaining one's own artistic vision and beliefs can entail a battle of wills. Such collaboration takes place not only among the actors onstage, but also with others involved in the performances: director, crew, costume designers, lighting designers, and so on. The collaboration between actors and audience is equally important. Last but not least, there is a collaboration between the actor and the text. In the words of Uta Hagen: "Theater is a communal adventure. . . . We must recognize that we need each other's strengths, and the more we need each other's professional comradeship, the better the chance we have of making theater. We must serve the play by serving each other; an ego-maniacal 'star' attitude is only self-serving and hurts everyone, including the 'star.'"[13]

The advice for theater aspirants offered by the veteran theater professionals was varied. Some encouraged young actors simply to get out there and try it; some encouraged them to apprentice themselves to a group; still others claimed that "the best thing someone can do is go to college and get a liberal arts degree, not get a theater degree." One experienced actor encouraged performers to attend graduate school, which would give them "the time to take themselves apart so that they could reintroduce themselves properly to the entertainment community." There is one aspect that all seemed to agree on, however: in the words of actor and educator Michael Chekhov, "The technique of acting can never be properly understood without *practicing* it."[14]

Meet the Theater Veterans

We began our study by interviewing twenty-one men and fifteen women involved in theater as actors, playwrights, artistic directors, and producers or executive directors (for further details, see the Appendix on Methods). These individuals were devoted to live theater and spurned the greater financial rewards of working in film or TV. The artistic directors worked in regional theaters connected to universities, led nonprofit theaters, took jobs on a freelance basis, or headed companies they themselves had established. All of the veteran theater professionals were deeply committed to and passionate about live theater. They embodied the sentiment expressed by Uta Hagen: "I pursued my work for love. Then, the fact that I was paid was incidental to the love. At best, being paid meant that I was taken seriously in this love of my work."[15]

For many of them, the goal of theater was to stimulate an audience by providing society with an image of itself. One playwright we interviewed said, "The goal of theater is to bring about some sort of societal change." Generally, the artists are trying to achieve such change by affecting individuals in personal ways. Other participants focus on the goal of theater as entertainment. If audiences are also provoked into questioning themselves and their world, this is a bonus. Some see theater as a ritualistic or spiritual experience. George Wolfe, director of the Public Theater in New York City, suggested that "theater . . . is really ultimately about ideas. . . . It's people sitting in the dark, watching people standing in the light, talking about the frailty of being a human. That's ultimately what it is, which is, to me, spiritual—which is ultimately what church should be and what any ritual should be." The role of the audience in this communion is pivotal. Oskar Eustis, director of the Trinity Repertory Company in Providence, Rhode Island, explained that theater requires "the physical presence of the audience. And as soon as you don't have an audience, it's not theater anymore." Without the reactions of those who observe the play, the rewards are minimal for actor, director, and playwright.

The veteran professionals in our study also endeavored to find and reveal truths through their involvement in theater: truths relating to the message of a text, authenticity in relationships among actors, or even faithfulness to one's self. Reaching these truths, however, always entails risk. Jack O'Brien, artistic director of the Old Globe Theatre in San Diego, commented: "I don't think that anything valuable happens unless you are willing to risk something." This risk is not thoughtless, nor is it easy. Actor and director André Gregory alluded to risk and the unknown: "I didn't say I loved it. I go kicking and screaming—but that is where I am forced to go." The theater professionals we interviewed believed that the reward was worth this effort. According to Emily Mann, artistic director of the McCarter Theatre in Princeton, New Jersey: "You are what you believe. And the more that you can jostle those beliefs and have people question themselves, and have a real dialogue with each other and themselves, . . . the further one grows as a human being." Perhaps as a result of the risks theater professionals must take, most expressed strong self-confidence as well as a sense of responsibility to themselves. Said stage actor Austin Pendleton: "The opportunity you give yourself to degrade yourself is so enormous that some huge self-protective thing helps you." Taking seriously this responsibility to self means pursuing work in which one believes, not compromising artistic vision.

In addition to the challenges of risk taking, the veteran professionals described the physical and emotional toll exacted by their commitment to theater. The work demands a flexible schedule. Often, professionals must travel for projects and work odd hours. Finding and sustaining meaningful personal relationships is a challenge, and for many with whom we spoke their colleagues had become in effect their family. Financial hardships were another obstacle, even for the established artists. One internationally respected actor and director commented that there had been "lots of times . . . when I couldn't see how if I continued to do what I do, I would be okay financially. Or if I continued to do what I do, I would have any money when I am older than I already am." André Gregory maintained that the artist should persevere regardless of financial hardships. But on further questioning, he acknowledged that it helped to have a wealthy father (as he did).

A majority of the veterans we interviewed were originally drawn to theater because they sought acceptance in some community. These artists found the support they were seeking, yet race and gender biases remained obstacles in their careers. All of the people of color and all of the women we interviewed referred to these challenges. Actor Cherry Jones pointed out that it was difficult for women over a certain age to find work in the United States. "People can become very bitter and I don't blame them. . . . Suddenly [you] are fifty years old and there's just nothing for you to do anymore." George Wolfe commented:

"There's a double standard for every single thing that I do because I am a person of color. Especially because I'm gay, but more because I'm a person of color. . . . It's why I have not received the credit that I deserve."

Rather than feeling defeated by the many hurdles they encounter, the theater professionals we interviewed saw these challenges as strengthening. David Dreyfoos, associate producer of the Oregon Shakespeare Festival, explained: "I don't look at anything as a negative. I only look at things as a positive, because you always can use something out of them. From any situation, you can always take something out of it and put a different bent on it and incorporate it into whatever the next thing you're moving into is." Many artists similarly view "mistakes" as opportunities for growth.

While the veteran theater professionals derived strength from their struggles, most were also uneasy about theater's future. Their concerns focused on escalating ticket prices and production costs, a dwindling and aging audience, and the limited availability of affordable performance space. With Broadway, off-Broadway, and regional theaters struggling to survive, many of the professionals agreed that new work will be highly dependent on small, not-for-profit venues. The veterans were also concerned that rising costs would discourage the casting of novice performers. Film or television celebrities are often placed in leading roles, as a way of inducing the public to buy expensive tickets. This successful marketing strategy may have the additional effect of lowering the expectations of the audience. Playwright Edward Albee reflected: "The likelihood of even fewer recondite—or apparently recondite—serious plays being done in the commercial theater grows all the time, because audiences have been trained to want less than they should want. They want safe, easy plays that do not disturb or upset. And so people who are going to make the money off of producing plays try to find the lowest common denominator."

A variety of factors make earning a livelihood in serious theater very difficult. Yet other venues for performance are thriving. According to the *Occupational Outlook Handbook* for 2002–2003 published by the U.S. Bureau of Labor Statistics, employment for actors, directors, and producers is expected to grow 21–35 percent through 2010, faster than the average for all occupations. As some workers leave the field because of the long hours, stiff competition, and low pay, demand for actors and production professionals will increase as both the foreign and domestic markets grow. In particular, the expansion of cable and satellite television, television syndication, home movie rentals, and music videos is creating demand for additional employees in entertainment fields. Attendance at stage productions is also expected to grow, and touring productions of Broadway plays and other large shows are providing new opportunities for actors and directors.[16]

Government support affects theater just as it does the field of genetics. A decline in government funding for the arts at the local, state, and national levels could constrain employment opportunities for stage actors, as opposed to those working in film or television. With so many talented aspirants in the profession, the competition for roles in theater is as fierce now as it has ever been. As in the past, only the most talented and dedicated actors will find regular employment.

According to the Actors Equity Association, the primary union for stage actors in the United States, young actors who were working on Broadway in 2001 could expect to earn a minimum salary of $1,252 per week. Those working in off-Broadway or smaller regional theaters generally earned between $440 and $551 per week, while actors working in regional theaters operating under an Equity agreement earned $500 to $728 per week. Actors appearing in traveling shows received, on average, $106 per day for living expenses.[17]

These seem like reasonable earnings, yet fewer than 15 percent of dues-paying Equity members work during any given week. In 1998, fewer than half worked onstage at all. In 2000, the average annual earnings for those able to find employment were less than $10,000.[18] The Screen Actors Guild reported an even lower figure for the average annual income its members earned from acting: $5,000. Clearly, salary for the typical actor is low; the handful of highly visible, highly paid celebrities constitutes the exception in theater. As we've seen, this uneven pattern of remuneration is also the case in journalism. Unlike the professions of journalism and genetics, however, theater offers employment on a much more erratic basis, and most actors must work in other occupations to survive financially.[19]

With these constraints and obstacles, why does acting draw more young people each year? One aspect may be the appeal of the lifestyle, which holds a possibility (however slight) of wealth and celebrity. Many children dream of seeing their name on a marquee and owning a private jet. And aspirants need not be academically or intellectually inclined in order to make fine performers, though personal understanding and an informed approach to the material at hand will obviously be relevant to the work.[20] In contrast to professionals working in journalism or genetics, those in theater can consider themselves participants in the field even if they act professionally for only a few weeks a year. This feature is especially attractive for young people worried about being "successful." There is always the hope that the big break is just around the corner. Actor and educator Adrian Cairns has pointed out that "adolescence is a time of impatience. Everything seems to take so long to happen—a short cut is immensely attractive. Some see theater and allied media as possibly offering such a short cut." But aspirants soon discover "just how much work, application, self-discipline, intelligence and cultural background is actually required to meet the competition from others with the same idea."[21]

The young actors in our study were driven by their deep passion for theater, regardless of the compensation or recognition they received. One young actor reflected:

Am I doing it for the money? Absolutely not. I found something that satisfies my soul. And there are people that tell
me, "Find something more stable." That's the only stable
thing that I see in my life. That's the only realistic thing I see
in my life. That's all I see myself doing. It's very hard for
people to understand that. I think that it's a gift. It's a gift to
find something in your life that you are so passionate about,
something that completes you, something that means more
to you than anything else, something that no matter what
I'm doing whether I've become known or not known. I
could be auditioning my whole life and then get that one
role in the theater, and that is [more] satisfying than any
other job that I could think of.

Echoing this sentiment, an articulate young Boston-based actor said:
"Theater is an oxygen supply. It's essential for me to go on."

Meet the Young Actors

For our study of young actors, we interviewed thirty-eight people:
twenty-one young professional actors who were completing their
training or launching their careers, and seventeen high school actors
who planned to commit themselves to the profession (for further details, see the Appendix on Methods). Like the geneticists with whom
we spoke, the actors were a diverse group in terms of their racial and
ethnic backgrounds. Yet similar themes emerged regarding their initial
involvement in theater, what kinds of individuals they were, the reasons that they persevered, and the tensions they encountered in the
profession.

Most of the young actors realized their interest in theater at a very
early age, often when they were as young as three or four. Though

many of the young journalists and geneticists in our sample reported their interest at a relatively early point in life, the actors seemed to be "born performers." Perhaps this difference in career precocity occurred because children require the fundamentals of reading and writing or an introduction to science to become involved in these more academic pursuits, while "make believe" requires no special instruction. A young Indian American actor recalled: "When I was young, I would sing a lot around the house. When I was two or three, I would pretend to carry a microphone." This inclination to perform endured throughout their lives. In our inventory of values, actors of all ages ranked "Creativity/Pioneering" and "Courage and Risk Taking" among their most important values.

Even those who did not report such early involvement in the domain pointed to the importance of having spent time alone in childhood developing and exercising the imagination necessary for theater. A twenty-five-year-old Jamaican Canadian actor told us:

> I spent a lot of time alone as a child, and I would sit in my room and just act out scenes. Like I wrote myself into that show "Facts of Life," and I was Tootsie's adopted sister. And her parents had died, and I was coming on the show because the parents were dead, but she didn't like me because I was adopted and I had to tell her that her parents had died. I mean, I had this whole thing arranged, and so I was acting out these scenes, and they were always very dramatic and very difficult and very emotional. And I think it was that desire for—well, the love of drama and the imagination, just pretend, make believe.

Most young people are drawn to theater because it looks like fun— a wonderful way to receive attention and recognition. One professional actor remembered: "When I was very little I wanted to be discovered, because it just sounded very exciting. I was really little and I'd heard that sometimes people were in grocery stores and then they just chose somebody. And so I would walk around the grocery store with little things for my mother, like, 'Look at this!' That kind of thing." All the young actors we interviewed loved to perform and to receive the subsequent recognition. Many high school actors continued to describe the lure of performance as the predominant draw. But when asked if this was still the appeal, college-age and young professional actors were more likely to say that as they had become deeply immersed in theater, they discovered the challenge of the work and grew to value the art and craft of theater rather than merely the recognition.

Only a few of the young actors indicated that they had found acceptance in theater that they were lacking elsewhere. Though they often described their drama clubs, conservatory cohort, or fellow cast members as feeling like a "family," very few said they felt as if they had not fit in with other children when growing up. In this respect they contrasted with their veteran counterparts, who often described being drawn to theater because they knew they were "different." Oskar Eustis, for example, said that in childhood "I did not feel like I fit in very well. . . . In the theater, I felt normal." Perhaps the younger actors did not have the years of perspective needed to judge why they had become involved in the domain. Or it may be that those actors who persisted and "made it" in theater were the ones who always felt separate from their contemporaries.

Several of the young actors described themselves as "sensitive." This was not a characteristic that the young journalists or geneticists used to describe themselves, and probably underscores the actors' emotional investment in their work. A seventeen-year-old actor commented: "[This] is also a quality that's important for an actor, to be sensitive. Because if you're so callous and you can never cry, how are you going to really get in touch with a character? How are you going to understand?" At the same time, she maintained that this acute sensitivity was "a drawback in personal life, wearing your heart on your sleeve." For sensitive people, theater may offer a safe, culturally sanctioned space in which to express the strong emotions they experience. Indeed, several of the actors with whom we spoke pointed to this aspect of theater as an initial draw. A thirty-year-old African American actor explained that the reason he had gone into theater work, "in all honesty, was to let out rage—yeah." He had grown up in a household that he described as "volatile"; it was "dangerous to get angry, because then you had a fight on your hands." As the youngest of eleven children, he said, "I chose my battles wisely." In theater, he finally had the opportunity to express his anger safely.

Whatever their sensitivity and vulnerability, all of the actors showed incredible discipline and determination to continue in their chosen profession. Their tenacity was staggering. They were sustained by their enjoyment of and passion for the work of acting itself, rather than by a promise of fame or wealth. In the inventory of values, at least one-quarter of the actors in each professional cohort included "Intrinsic Motivation/Enjoyment of the Activity" as one of their top four personal values as individuals. Young professional actors were also marked by a tremendous confidence in their own talent and ability to succeed. An actress finishing her college-level conservatory training said: "I think ever since I started . . . there was a sense of, 'Well, I hope I'm recognized as much as I should be.' . . . I hadn't fully understood the potential of my abilities, but there was a sense of 'I know I'm going to greatness, but I don't know how to—I hope I get there, I hope I get my greatness.' . . . And I guess that's ambition; I think I'm very ambitious and I always was ambitious."

A striking 90 percent of the young professional actors expressed an optimistic approach to their life and work. This sense of optimism for navigating work-related obstacles was not evidenced by the journalists and geneticists with whom we spoke, perhaps because they were less prepared for the hardships of their chosen professions. While many of the actors described themselves as having been optimistic since childhood, they also pointed out the advantages of this attitude as a survival strategy. A twenty-two-year old black Canadian actor said: "There's no reason why I can't do whatever it is. You know, I'm competent, my limbs are working, thank God, and whatever. . . . Even if it feels very far away from me, if I really want to get there, if I work, I can get there, you know, I can find it."

Most of the actors we interviewed gave the impression that they could not help choosing acting as a profession. They needed to express themselves, and several claimed that they were not qualified for anything else. When we spoke with a gifted Boston-based high school actor about the profession he had already chosen, he said: "If asked to define what it is prematurely, I couldn't verbalize it. If I could, I wouldn't act. I do what I do because there is no other way to express myself. Writing it down or speaking it would be a good deal easier if I could manage it." He was going into acting, he claimed, "because I couldn't do anything else. . . . There is no way, fairly much, to live comfortably as a practitioner. So it isn't whether you succeed or not. . . . There's no way to live comfortably in this business. Meaning that the only reason you would do it was if there was no other way. Every true artist, I think, approaches it with this same desperation. Which is submitting to it. It's a passion, and a passion is passive, and passivity is something overwhelming."

Beyond the ambition they derived from the work itself, the young actors mentioned other motivating factors. Most frequently, like the journalists and geneticists, the aspiring actors said they had supportive parents (though few had "stage moms"). In fact, some had originally been inspired to work in theater because they had parents who were artists themselves. Others came from families where art was not emphasized. Most often, the actors said their families provided role models of hard work and dedication. In cases of significant parental support, the help came in multiple forms: transportation, rehearsing and memorizing lines, and handling difficult directors.

Various other role models—such as mentors (older peers, professors, sometimes even significant others) and teachers—were mentioned as being supportive, though they sometimes offered "tough love." Interestingly, the director of a high school arts academy regularly discouraged her students from pursuing acting professionally—not an uncommon practice on the part of the theater educators with whom we spoke. The actors themselves cautioned potential aspirants that if there was any other career they could pursue, they should not go into acting.

The high school actors were likely to mention that they had friends in theater who were supportive. Many of these actors became involved in theater work so that they could spend time with friends, or a boyfriend or girlfriend, and then they ended up getting "hooked." Frequently, the high school actors said that in other respects they felt at odds with the school community. In theater, they found like-minded peers and a sense of belonging. Actors in all three of our age groups frequently selected "Rewarding and Supporting Relationships" as a principal value, with the trend increasing over the course of their careers and their lives.

Voicing a sentiment not heard from journalists or geneticists, the young actors often said that their work was a spiritual oasis. Theater was a "spiritual thing," said one high school actor, "It's where I get my peace." And the young professional actors placed greater emphasis on the value of "Spirituality" in their work than the high school actors or the veteran theater professionals. Several of the budding professionals spoke of theater as their "church" or "sanctuary." Other young actors mentioned the importance of community, communication, or communion, either in relation to or separately from this notion of theater as a sacred space. Even those who did not describe theater as a sanctuary indicated that theater was important in the formation of ties to others. Unfortunately, this sanctuary was not enough to protect young actors from the brutality of theater as a business.

Personal and Professional Tradeoffs

Though acting can be tremendously rewarding, it is a grueling business and young aspirants confront countless obstacles. The individuals with whom we spoke told us of the difficulties they had maintaining relationships with friends and family, making ends meet financially, and performing for audiences who wanted only to be passively entertained instead of challenged by new ideas.

The decision to make a career in theater shaped each individual's personal life. Of the twenty-one young professionals we interviewed, only two were married, only a handful were in serious intimate relationships, two were divorced, and one had recently ended an engagement. At least one divorce and the broken engagement were specifically linked to the fact that the individuals gave greater priority to their theater work than to their relationships. An actor explained why she got divorced: "I have to do this work and it's a part of who I am, and I feel it's a part of why I'm on this planet. And it is where I feel often the most alive and feel like I have the strongest voice. And I am most who I am when I am acting, and it has to be there to the neglect or to the exclusion of all else if necessary, I guess. . . . it's really tough, and it makes me really question what is possible in terms of relationships in this business."

On the other hand, an unusually accomplished high school actor and director objected to the notion of separating work from a personal life: "Why can't you love what you do? Why isn't your work your play?

Why aren't the relationships that you have worth more than relaxation?" Perhaps this holistic view of the actor's life made him more accepting of its demands than were his older counterparts, who were often torn as they sought to balance different priorities. The need to "create balance in one's life" was more often cited by the young professionals than by the high school actors.

Like their counterparts in journalism and genetics, the actors we interviewed were torn between maintaining integrity to their personal values and fulfilling their ambition in theater. Across the three professional stages, the theater professionals consistently ranked "Honesty and Integrity" and "Quality of Work" as values that were very important in their work lives. Because the actors felt so strongly about upholding these values in their work, the effort to maintain honesty, integrity, and quality in their work while fulfilling their ambitions—or just paying the rent—was that much more challenging.

Some challenges were specific to particular groups. For example, almost all of the people of color we interviewed (ten out of eleven young professionals) said they had encountered racially demeaning roles. Ironically, many of them said they had difficulty getting cast in their own ethnic or racial group because they didn't fit the casting directors' stereotypes. A Jamaican Canadian actor talked about her struggle to find roles that did not focus on her race. Sometimes, she said, she was not even given the opportunity to audition for roles, because of the color of her skin: "I think that's the hardest thing for me, because I feel like that's the hardest to control. That's the hardest to get around."

Both the women and men whom we interviewed mentioned the poor treatment of women in theater. Specifically, they spoke of issues ranging from pressure to appear nude onstage to the scarcity of good roles for women over fifty. One Korean American conservatory student offered his perspective:

I think that a lot of people in this business tend to do things that go against their moral values or their integrity or their dignity. And they do that so they can get that break, you know? Women, especially. It just really makes me sort of sad that the business is geared towards this type of objectificat- ion, . . . to know that there are hundreds—hundreds of women in L.A., . . . aspiring actors, that they know that they do not want to appear in the nude in anything, but they do, and they are miserable while they do it, just to get that break.

The way actors choose to respond to these challenges may depend on the context. How badly do they need the money? How well con- nected is the director? What do they need to take their career to the next level? What are the lines that they would never cross—and why?

"My Son the Actor?" (Living with Authority)

All of the actors we interviewed discussed their parents. Most of the high school and young professional actors said that their greatest source of support was encouragement from their parents. Still, few of them said their parents hoped that their offspring would pursue acting as a career. Even parents who were supportive of acting as a career usu- ally expressed apprehension at the prospect, especially because of the emotional and financial challenges their offspring would face.

Some of the actors said their parents did not view acting as a wor- thy career. Perhaps the parents feared that their children would fall into what they perceived as the unethical or immoral behavior charac- teristic of the profession. Inaccurate stereotypes of actors were ram- pant; for example, some of the actors said their parents thought that all theater professionals were gay or lesbian, sexually permissive, and drug dependent.

Rob, a seventeen-year-old white actor living in a predominantly blue-collar town in northeastern Massachusetts, faced a great deal of opposition from his father. Rob had played his first role in second grade because acting was a "cool" thing to do at his school. He liked his first taste of being in front of the audience and continued to be involved in theater activities, though he pointed out that in high school "it's definitely not the cool thing to do anymore." In fact, "if you do anything artsy, you are either ignored completely or any attention you receive is completely negative." Although teenagers generated much of the negative reaction to theater, he said, the entire town seemed to look down on theater. Students' sports teams and other extracurricular activities were publicly funded, but the high school drama club received no financial support. The fact that the drama club had to raise its own money made acting even more enjoyable for Rob: he knew "that everything on the show was done by everyone on the show. It wasn't just handed to us."

Rob was drawn to theater because of the audience: "You feel like you are doing something good for them too, because they are getting the entertainment." He also valued the way acting allowed him to step outside of his own life and become someone else for a while. He was passionate about theater and felt that it fulfilled a basic need: "I need to perform . . . because that is just what I do and who I am. And I cannot do anything else. My goal is to become a performer so I don't have to do anything else. . . . If I am not performing and I can't perform, a huge part of me is taken away. It's in my blood to go up onstage and do what I can to entertain an audience. . . . It is like eating or sleeping or something. It is part of my existence."

Several years prior to our interview, Rob's father had tried to redirect him toward activities that were more conventional for boys in their town. His father was very strict, Rob said: "It was his way or no way." During Rob's first year of high school, his father forced him to attend a vocational school specifically because it had no theater program. His father, said Rob, was "really into image." In their town, "the proper image to have is that you go to work from nine to five, you come home, and everyone's a happy family. Your sons play football or hockey, and your daughter sings and takes dance." Rob did not want to play football or hockey, and his father deplored his lack of conformity. Likewise, Rob's stepmother told him that theater was "a waste of time." Though Rob was briefly allowed to be involved with a community theater, one year prior to our interview Rob's father had told him that he could no longer be involved with theater at all. For six months Rob avoided all theater activities, sinking into a deep depression. Finally he ended this hiatus (against his father's wishes) and was cast in a high school production. When his father again forbade him to participate, Rob moved out of the house.

Interestingly, Rob's father had himself been seriously involved in theater for many years, and had even performed in one professional show. Rob did not know why his father had stopped acting, but speculated that "he was just worried that he wasn't going to be able to make it." His grandmother, he said, thought that his father was discouraging Rob out of jealousy: "My grandmother said the reason he didn't want me to go into theater as a career is because I had the ambition he didn't have to do it." Despite his father's opposition, Rob decided to major in musical theater at a prestigious conservatory program.

Rob was able to sustain his passion for theater in spite of the obstacles his family and community presented. He maintained a responsibility to self which entailed sacrificing a responsibility to others—in this case, his father and stepmother. We did not speak with Rob's father, and can only speculate as to why he was so set against his son's involvement in theater. And it is impossible to tell whether this opposition helped to solidify Rob's commitment to theater. All we can report is that Rob chose to pursue what he believed to be his mission as an actor.

Parental resistance was not unusual in the families of young actors. The father of one aspiring actor limited her college choices to Ivy League schools. When she told him that Harvard did not have a theater major, he responded, "They're smart because they know what really is good in academics." She chose to attend Dartmouth because they had a small but highly respected theater program.

The clash between skeptical parent and passionate offspring may be characteristic of the high school years. The parents of the young professionals we interviewed had often come to accept and support their children's career choice. The parents of one young Korean American actor, whom we'll call Jane, were at first strongly opposed to her pursuing a career in theater. On the opening night of her high school production of *Oklahoma!* her mother came backstage, grabbed her by the arm, and said, "How could you embarrass me like that? . . . You're Korean—you don't belong in *Oklahoma!*" While this was a traumatic experience for Jane, it also strengthened her resolve to continue in theater. Throughout her high school years, she said, her parents had ignored her involvement in theater because "performance was not really allowed and not acknowledged as a legitimate pursuit." She recalled being upset with her mother and asking why her parents couldn't be supportive. Her mother responded, "If you're doing this because you want people to approve of you, then you should just quit now." At this point Jane realized that her mother simply wanted to protect her from the harsh life of being an artist. After Jane finished high school, she played the Buddha in a production of *Journey to the West* at the Goodman Theater in Chicago. Because Jane's family is devoutly Zen Buddhist, this experience, she said, "won them over in some sort of weird way," and henceforth they were supportive of her work.

When it came to relations with authority figures outside the family, the actors with whom we spoke said they faced many challenges in dealing with their directors—the individuals who ultimately controlled their work. Even if they did not agree with their directors' decisions and interpretations about a script or a character, the actors needed to listen to their directors. Disagreeing or arguing with a director could be seen as violating the collaborative spirit—one of the most essential elements of theater. One high school actor explained, "There's definitely been times when I wished that I could take a play a certain way. . . . A lot of it's out of your control. The director has the ability to change the big picture, and if you don't do what the director wants, you are just going to look like you're not a member of the play." So it was in an actor's best interest to live with the frustration and not complain to others. Like the lab advisors of young scientists, directors have the power and influence to derail an actor's career: power is magnified because there is only a small network of professional agents, casting directors, and acting directors in any particular city. One young actor told us that for this reason she would never argue with a director or let others know she was upset, for that would be "shooting myself in the foot."

The veteran professionals said they had once faced this dilemma themselves. Critically acclaimed actor Joan Allen described an incident at the start of her film career. A director had decided to use live ammunition to blow out the windows in a house. No one was hurt during the event, but bullets had ricocheted off trucks in which the film's cast and crew were sitting. Allen had been troubled that the director had created such a dangerous situation for the actors and crew. She had discussed the incident with others, but she had never spoken to the director about her concern. One reason for this, she told us, might have been her tendency as an actor to give the director almost "too much power." She was likely to assume "that he knows what he's doing," or to say to herself, "He's the one that's in charge." Later in her career, she became more forthright about her needs and limitations. No doubt this was because she became a known and valuable commodity, and thus the risk to her career decreased.

This tension between collaboration and concession was expressed by many of the young actors. A student at the Yale School of Drama explained: "To me, [good collaboration is] when there isn't a hierarchy . . . when people are treated equally, basically, and that there's enough time for people to participate fully if they wish." This ideal is difficult to achieve, of course, and many of the actors we interviewed spoke of tensions with peers.

"There's No 'I' in 'Team'" (Living with Others)

A young actor whom we'll call Jesse had been deeply involved with theater since the age of ten. His inclination was warmly welcomed by his parents—indeed, his father was initially an actor, then a director and then a producer. Jesse's parents helped him pursue his passion for a theater career in every way they could. As a result of his father's personal involvement in the business, his parents' financial support, and the experience of growing up in theater-rich New York City, Jesse was an astute actor. He knew what it took to become a successful professional.

Through his own experiences at selective summer theater programs, in theater workshops outside of school, and at the famed Fiorello H. LaGuardia High School of Music and Art and Performing Arts, Jesse learned first-hand not only about methods and skills, but also about the importance of collaboration. He singled out collaboration as one of the most intriguing and rewarding aspects of theater: "I love [theater] so much. Theater is the most collaborative art. You have a set designer, a costume designer, a lighting designer, a director; you have a composer and lyricist. . . . And then you have all of these actors, and you are all working towards a common goal, but you are all fitting your pieces together." He explained further: "So if there's any kind of tension or hostility in that, it's really difficult. And that's why I think you have to be nice in the business. And that's something like they try to teach you as well. You have to be competitive, but you have to be kind."

Jesse had experienced the enormous tension between competitiveness and collaboration. At LaGuardia High School, he and his fellow students spent three years working together—honing their skills, learning different philosophies and methods, and developing characters through their work on collaborative scenes. Not until senior year did they have the opportunity to audition for a show—and this process, Jesse informed us, was purposeful. At the end of senior year, when the students were learning whether they had been admitted to colleges or conservatories and whether they would be entering theater professionally, LaGuardia hosted an annual Spring Drama Festival—three plays in repertoire, for which everyone auditioned. The stakes were high in these auditions: these were the only productions a student had a chance to be in during his entire high school career, and professional agents would come to the festival to scout actors. Jesse described this intensity:

> The irony is that senior year, all of a sudden you're having to be really competitive. . . . Everybody auditions for that and goes through callback processes together, and all of a sudden it's not, you know, the same as working in your studio acting class, where everybody has a scene and everybody is going to have equal time. And not everybody gets into [a show]. [The directors] actually choose the people they want to show to the industry. . . . That kind of changes the environment. . . . You are up against people, and really up against them. Like

they could really get this part over you, that you thought you were, like, way better than freshman year.

Jesse viewed this process as preparation for the real world of theater; he knew that the issues of competition and collaboration with peers would pervade the professional sphere. In addition, he understood that once cast in a show, he would need to display cooperation, loyalty, and dedication to the collaborative effort. Jesse related one particular situation in which a peer chided him for his lack of effort. It was a confrontation that nearly caused the demise of the entire production.

In the Spring Drama Festival, Jesse was fortunate to be cast in two different shows—a striking affirmation of his talent. His first show was a draining experience. Although he loved the script and the director, the time he devoted to the production was exhausting. Because the show was so complicated technically, rehearsals took twelve hours every day. Jesse did not mind. He looked forward to going to rehearsals every day, and told us that "it was one of the best experiences I ever had," mostly due to the director. But the second show he was involved in was not of the same caliber. Jesse became involved in the second show right after finishing the first, and two months after the second had begun rehearsals. He said that the new play was "less successful" for him, in large part because of the director. "I felt like I had to work too hard to make the material work, because . . . I didn't understand where she wanted it to go. And I didn't understand what she was trying to accomplish. Her vision wasn't clear, except to make it funny. . . . But that's not enough."

Jesse was tired, both physically and emotionally. "They were just about to start their hell time, which I had just finished. So I was going from like three, four weeks of hell time into three, four weeks of hell time. And I really didn't want to be there. And so for the first week I just watched and I would say like really negative things about it." Jesse did not want to participate in this second show for two reasons: first, sheer exhaustion; and second, fear that the show would not come together and might ultimately tarnish his reputation as an actor.

A few weeks into rehearsals, one of the actors, who was a close friend, approached Jesse and said that the whole cast had been feeling a "negative vibe" since he joined. She admitted, "We know that we have a lot to work on . . . and we know that it's not the best thing in the world, but the only thing we have going for us is our spirit. And we feel like since you've gotten here, there's been a very tense atmosphere." Jesse told us that this confrontation "really hit me." He had not realized that his behavior was having such a negative impact on people, or that his lack of energy and his indifference were affecting the rest of the cast.

Jesse learned his lesson. "No one will ever have to tell me that again. Because I now see—because people and actors are very sensitive anyway, so even if you think . . . you're hiding your feelings you are probably not, because everybody is ultrasensitive anyway. . . . You have to be . . . very in tune to the environment, and what's around you. . . . It was a very awakening experience because it made me think, 'If this was professional and they were feeling that, I probably would have been fired already.'"

In the descriptions provided by our subjects, the tensions inherent in collaboration took a number of forms. Because the actors needed to spend time developing their characters and learning the lines and cues for their particular roles, the balance between autonomy and collaboration was often precarious for them. They discussed the importance of autonomy in various contexts. Some of them said that the time they had spent alone as children had fostered their facility in creating the imaginary inner worlds on which they drew in their work. Others mentioned the importance of responsibility to self by following a healthy diet or by advocating for one's own career. Yet the work that they did in isolation was ultimately brought to their collaborative work in theater.

A Boston-based teenage actor defined the opposite of collaboration: "Sleaze. When I say 'sleaze,' I mean it's selfishness." This selfishness was evident in "actors in a production upstaging other actors, . . . and then that results in a production's catastrophe." In his opinion, selfishness was the opposite of collaboration, because theater was "such a group effort—or in fact maybe the miraculous thing about theater is that it's the only artistry that takes such a company of people to produce." Those who tried to garner audience attention for themselves at the expense of the production, he believed, were "depriving themselves of that, that feeling—those multiple brushstrokes contributing." Not only would the actor be denying himself the experience of contributing to the production; he would also be failing in his responsibility to others by leaving his colleagues unsupported and vulnerable onstage.

Jessica, a twenty-one-year-old actor completing her undergraduate training at Boston University, described one frustrating situation during which she felt little support from a fellow actor. She was performing in a show in which she played the role of "a two-year-old [in] this little Scottish group of children. And we were called in the text 'the brood.' So we were just this mass group." After working well together in rehearsals, the group performed the play at the university's student matinee. Rather than working as part of the ensemble, Jessica said, "one of the brood members just started 'shmacting'—like, just started hamming a lot of things."

> I remember feeling a real sense of abandonment. . . . First of all, it took me out of the role of the play. There is, I think, a real trust that goes on when you go in it together. . . . And I

see people in the student matinee change a little bit, . . . give
it a little bit to the audience more than we've worked or than
we have in every other show. And it's not necessarily a bad
thing, but I think it's too easy. I do, I feel like "Shame on
you"—I think it's an abandonment.

The ideal of collaboration, she believed, is "a real generosity to the
moment. . . . There's a lack of ego too." Another young actor remarked that it was "the duty of every actor to contribute as much as
they possibly can to a production's success. Meaning the entire production's success." For this reason, one graduating high school senior
who was planning to pursue acting professionally had chosen the college he wanted to attend based on how comfortable he felt in the
groups he encountered. He described the experience of being at the
school he ultimately selected: "I sat in on a class. . . . I was sitting in
the back, and they said, 'No, come here, sit with us.' You know, that's
really unique in this business, from everything I understand and from
the people that I've talked to."

So far, we have described the way in which the actors in our study
coped with external pressures—those stemming from authority figures
and peers. But they also had to wrestle with internal promptings.
They had to monitor whether their behaviors and actions were aligned
with the kind of person—and worker—they wanted to be. As they
struggled to make ends meet, the aspiring young actors often faced
professional choices that risked compromising their personal values—
for example, being offered a paying role with no aesthetic worth, or
getting a part at a well-known theater company that held policies in
conflict with the actor's personal values. One high school actor commented: "When financial stability can be the absence of emotional
stability, it's too much of a price." The decision to compromise personal integrity for ambition or money was not usually made lightly,

but it was often the outcome. We heard thoughts on such a choice from a twenty-five-year-old woman we'll call Meg, an Asian American actor who faced a difficult decision on whether to accept a role that portrayed her race in a unfavorable way.

"Your Money or Your Soul" (Living with Self)

Meg had initially been attracted to theater as a way of finding her "voice." Asian Americans, she thought, had long been scarce in theater, and this lack had fueled her ambition. In childhood, she said, "I didn't see very many Asian American people on television, and I didn't really have any figures to identify with, like voices that I could identify with. I felt very underrepresented from a very early age." Through her work in theater, she said, she wanted to demonstrate that Asian American women could be versatile, and thus to dispel the myths of the geisha girl and the dragon lady. "To see that Asian Americans aren't represented properly by the dominant media or by commercial media really drives my work." Yet Meg had little financial support. Sometimes she compromised her values to take a role that would provide some income or a part that would help to advance her career. "I know sometimes I may have to bend those rules a little and justify things, because I need to pay my rent."

Several years prior to our interview, Meg had taken a leading role in a prestigious play. The role was a superficial stereotype of Asian women, but she agreed to do it because the director was well known and well connected in the theater world.

> [The play] was poorly written, and the dialect too was incorrect. It was written in a broken Japanese-English kind of dialect. I didn't know what it was; it wasn't Japanese. And the story was like the classic—it was like *Madame Butterfly*, it was like this self-sacrificing Asian woman. But I got offered

the role; I auditioned for the role and I got it, and I dealt with the ignorances of the director and the writer. It was just this very fantasized view of what they thought an Asian woman or an Asian relationship was like.

Meg believed she had been condemned by her community for taking a role that portrayed Asian American women in a stereotypical way. At the same time, in order to succeed and survive as an actress, she felt she had to accept some of these roles. And ultimately, like many of the journalists and geneticists we interviewed, she indicated that she thought the ends justified the means. In this case, taking substandard roles that could bring greater opportunities would allow her to gain power in the theater community and ultimately to realize her most cherished values.

Meg contended that as she gained influence, she would be in a better position to undermine racial stereotypes. For her, the expectation of taking a principled stand in the future warranted compromises in the present:

> So I could get panned by people in my community, in the Asian American community, for selling out. But I think in the end, my goals—what I want to achieve in the end betters, I think, my racial situation in this country. . . . That's my aim. Like, I do plan to break past a lot of the stereotypes. And a lot of—particularly the stereotypes that oppress us in theater. But I also recognize what power is, and I recognize I'm sort of fighting from the inside up, you know what I mean? I know there are different ways to go about it. There are some people who think you need to tear down the old institutions before you can ever effect change. I'm not convinced of that.

For the time being, at least, Meg's sacrifice of personal integrity and aesthetic standards seemed to be producing the outcome she had hoped for: the director admired her work, and the part led to other roles. She got the opportunity to perform with a highly respected organization, and she continued to use the director as a reference. In fact, she was accepted into a prestigious acting program in part because of this director's excellent recommendation. Discussing her strategy for portraying a role she found wanting, she said: "I tried to bring as much dignity to that role as I possibly could. But I didn't try to save her play because I wanted it to be bad." She participated purely for the sake of "getting a good reference," though she accomplished this goal at some cost to her personal integrity and possibly to her moral standing in her community. She did not know whether the choice would pay off in the long term or whether she would have to make further ethical sacrifices.

There were actors in our study who framed the issue of typecasting in other ways. Another young Asian American actor we interviewed said that while she tried to maintain her own sense of integrity, there ultimately could be no hard and fast rules for actors. Sometimes one had to operate on a number of levels simultaneously:

> You really don't know how you're going to feel about something or how you're going to react to something. . . . There have been other kinds of roles where I thought, "Oh, my God, that's totally stereotyped. That's so humiliating." But at the end of the day, that might not have totally been the case, because there was a kind of complexity and nuance to it that I think I might have overreacted to, or whatever. . . . I guess my point is that I have found that often those rules that I cling to have failed me, ultimately, because it's very difficult then and sometimes impossible to plan for those

kinds of things. And I think that the best preparation for those situations is to just really know yourself as much as possible and to live in the truth of yourself and not lie to yourself. So that when you're in a situation, you know if something is a lie—like, you feel it in your body, you just know when you're lying to yourself or when you're negotiating with yourself so you can get what you think you want.

Meg's compromise was similar in some respects to that of the young journalist Karen, discussed in Chapter 2. Karen admitted that she had misrepresented herself to sources in order to gain the most accurate information; in a sense, Meg was also misrepresenting herself—her beliefs and values—with the aim of furthering her career as well as the situation of her racial group. Meg's view seemed to be that the choices she made in the present to nurture her ambition—sometimes at the expense of her integrity—would ultimately bring a greater reward: she would eventually be able to gratify her sense of responsibility to herself (her integrity and ambition), as well as her sense of responsibility to her community. She was calculating that her short-term gains in career milestones would position her to wield greater public influence. Whether she and her community could live with her choices without damage was unclear.

Traversing Ethical Faultlines

To flesh out the testimony gathered in our interviews, we also looked closely at how the young actors—at two different points in their professional careers—conceived of various responsibilities and ethical issues. Perhaps the strongest conclusion we can draw from our study is that the actors felt an overwhelming sense of integrity or responsibility to self. A healthy majority of the high school and professional actors spoke of feeling a sense of responsibility to do what they loved and a comparable sense of responsibility to carry out work that met their own personal definition of high quality. The young actors felt that if they remained passionate about their work and fully committed to this passion, they would be able to surmount any challenge. A seventeen-year-old LaGuardia student actor expanded on the idea of responsibility to self: "If you get rejected by the thing you hold dear, if you hold the public dearest and you don't get a job for two years, you'll lose your passion. And that's like your parents disowning you. I think that if you trust yourself more than you do society as a whole, then it will be good."

Some of the actors discussed responsibility to self in terms of their physical appearance. One strikingly attractive student at Boston University said she might consider having plastic surgery in order to fit into a more conventional idea of beauty. This intervention would make her feel that she had given all she could to "make it" in theater: "It really just comes down to asking yourself, 'What do I really want here?' Because if what you really, really want is to be successful, then no one is going to look at you and tell you that being gorgeous is going to hurt. Like if you can get that body, you're increasing your chances of success, I think. If that's what you want, then it's valid . . . and maybe getting plastic surgery doesn't interfere."

Other actors said they would fit themselves as best they can, short of surgery, into a conventional sense of beauty in order to do commercial work. But some would not even consider acting in commercials. Instead, they chose to wait on tables, do office work, or take proofreading jobs to pay the bills, and continued to participate in productions that they believed in, based on their merit and "with warts and all." Still other actors we interviewed wrote plays and started theater companies to create their own work, and to develop the kinds of roles they wanted to play.

In comparison to individuals in other professions, the actors stood out in their insistence on a sense of responsibility to others. The actors felt indebted to the cast, crew, and ensemble, because without those people there would be no show. This allegiance to colleagues was sometimes illustrated in remarkable ways. An eighteen-year-old acting student attending high school in Brookline, Massachusetts, explained that his involvement in theater had caused him to break up with his girlfriend. "I think what ultimately broke that relationship up was that I [had become] more responsible to her rather than to things that were more important to me." Rather than allow his responsibility to theater to be compromised by his relationship, he ended the relationship. Aside from the colleagues and peers with whom the actors worked most closely, both the high school and young professionals expressed a responsibility to the audience. One eighteen-year-old student at LaGuardia High School said the audience was inspiring her to a career in theater: "There's a message I think I want to give to the audience. But at the same time it's not like I'm dominating them. It's almost like a partnership that you have with them." Some of the actors with whom we spoke said they felt a responsibility to the audience because the audience is what kept theater alive—these were the people that paid for tickets and brought their energy to the playhouse. Just as the journalists were interested in serving their readers, the actors said they would not be performing if there were no audience.

The one marked difference in the ways actors at different points in their careers expressed responsibility was in terms of their sense of obligation to the domain of theater. Like the veteran actors, nearly three-quarters of the emerging professionals expressed a responsibility to the domain, but fewer than one-fifth of the high school actors did so. Indeed, only a few high school students even differentiated between the stage and other media. Those who did assert a specific responsibility to live theater had often been exposed to it at an early age, mainly because they grew up in New York City. But at the same time, out of necessity, these young professionals were seeking ways to maneuver through the wider world of acting as a profession. We deliberately sought actors who were dedicated to live theater as opposed to film or TV, but even the most dedicated of the young actors we interviewed were willing to try other media—as one student remarked, "particularly now, with all my student loans to pay off."

Many of the actors maintained that the mission of theater is to bring social problems to light in a compelling way. The British actor Simon Callow has written: "All theatre, in any case, . . . is inevitably political. It *always* makes a statement even if that statement is only: 'Isn't bourgeois life wonderful?'"[22] The effects of theater on the public, however, are generally indirect rather than immediate. Nor does theater usually inform the public of a threatening situation or indeed pose a threat, as may happen, respectively, in the areas of journalism and genetics. Thus, while theater professionals across our three groups cited ethical and moral concerns for their work, we did not use an ethics survey to study differences among the groups. Nonetheless, three issues of ethical concern emerged with sufficient frequency to represent a trend:

1. Limited aesthetic quality of the work (the actors felt pressured to compromise the quality of their work);
2. Roles that degraded the actors themselves or others (the actors felt ambivalent about taking roles that promoted a racial or gender stereotype, or hatred toward a particular group);
3. Directors' abuse of power.

The professionals on the brink of their careers expressed more concern than the high school actors about each of these issues. For example, fewer than a quarter of the high school actors—compared to two-thirds of the young professional actors—articulated concern around representations of race. Like the "cocooned" high school journalists, the younger actors can be seen as working in a more protected, less market-driven environment. (It may be relevant, as well, that the young professionals in our sample were more racially diverse than the high school actors.) Still, the majority of young professionals of all races with whom we spoke were intensely troubled about taking roles that demeaned a particular race, and about the fact that theater in the United States does not fairly represent racial diversity. A twenty-one-year-old white student, a senior at Boston University, remarked on the lack of diversity both onstage and in the audience:

> I think that theater currently, just as a generalization, doesn't necessarily represent all of the masses. I think it responds in a lot of ways to a certain class of people, a certain race of people. I think it is only made accessible to certain groups of people. . . . So I'd like to see a more diversified audience. I'd like to see more color in the audiences. I think a lot of audiences, whenever I look around, [are] mostly white, middle-aged people—unless you're in a specific area that's responding to a specific group of people.

Similarly, far more young professionals than high school actors expressed ethical concerns related to the position of women in theater. Since there were fewer parts available for women than for men, the women with whom we spoke often felt they had to compromise themselves to get any role at all. This might mean fulfilling the negative stereotype of African American women by playing a prostitute, or trying to attain the conventional physical ideal through liposuction. Although none of the actors described anyone who had "slept their way to the top," several of the women said they had felt pressured or ill at ease when working with men. One said she felt uncomfortable working with a particular male director ("The guy was really creeping me out because he was very touchy"), and another recalled she had felt physically unsafe with a certain male colleague. One young actor said that women, especially, had to "be aware if there are any lines being crossed"; yet she also acknowledged that "there's something about when people are casting. . . . Finding that other person attractive is really important. And so it's usually in the mix somewhere." Actors, she said, "know that that's something that's going to be used to your advantage, to be appealing or, at times, to be sexy or charm the pants off of some artistic director, or something. . . . And so I think that we're all, as women, just aware of the vibes that we're getting."

Nearly two-thirds of the high school actors did express ethical concern about participating out of financial need in productions with limited aesthetic value out of financial need. All of these student actors acknowledged that it was difficult to "make it" as an actor, but they were sure they would not compromise their professional standards for money. One precocious sixteen-year-old Boston-based actor remarked:

> Well, money and theater are two very separate things which, when they are intertwined, aren't done so very well. And if I was in a position where money was required, I wouldn't look to the work to be the source of it. There's several other things that a person can do, things of higher morality than a pornography shoot, for instance, which isn't acting. . . . Art is always something that I do for . . . its artistic standards' sake, and never something that I would do for money.

Generally, the students seemed already to have developed theories and methods for dealing with such situations. This was true particularly for the students at LaGuardia High School, where part of their training was preparing them for the professional world. All of the students took a class called "Career Management," in which various actors and directors would come to talk to them about the "business":

how to audition, how to write a cover letter, how to sign with an agent. LaGuardia students were not allowed to participate in theater work outside of school until their senior year. One student commented that after her own experience of being pressured by a director, she understood why the institution did not support students' work in the professional world until they had graduated. She had been asked to do something inappropriate for a short film she was making on the side, and felt she could not say no to the director. Though she had thought she was ready to work professionally, she realized "you think you know, but you have no idea. You don't know. You don't know what's important to you, and you could get yourself into trouble just like I almost did. . . . LaGuardia has helped me [with] not only learning about acting, learning about the business, learning about the types of people in the business."

Outside the protective environment of the school, the actors would inevitably be faced with difficult decisions. Even taking union-sanctioned breaks could get a young actor into trouble. A young actor commented that "sometimes people forget. That's fine, but sometimes it's taken advantage of. Just actors in general are perceived as, 'Well, they love what they do, so they don't mind working hours upon hours.'" On several occasions he had been the one to say, "'Look, we need a break. Just give us a break and we'll come back and do this, but we need a break. I need a break to function properly.'" He took a stand, but did so to his own detriment because "people don't take to that too kindly or they think that I might be causing trouble, and then I have to go back afterwards and apologize." In one case, before he had smoothed the situation over, his fellow actors stopped speaking to him. The risk of standing up for what should be an actor's right could be costly: "This business is so much on your name and how you're perceived as a worker—Are you a good worker? Are you a trouble-maker? or whatever—that I can't be perceived as a troublemaker, because that doesn't help, even though I need to stick up for what I am. So there are consequences, but I have to smooth them over afterwards, or somehow come back and be okay to prove that I am a good worker."

Probably because the veteran professionals were more established and often in positions of power themselves, fewer than half of them raised ethical concerns during our interviews. These professionals worried less about whether the next opportunity was coming, and were aware of the power they possessed. When they encountered ethical dilemmas about how to maintain their professional integrity, these entailed different repercussions. Specifically, veterans who expressed ethical concerns commonly described situations in which they had to decide whether to satisfy their own needs at the risk of harming others' opportunities, or to compromise their own values and desires for the sake of helping those with whom they worked. An established playwright said she sometimes reached the point where she asked, "Why am I obligated to make a decision that's bad for my career just to help your career?" The costs of refusing to compromise artistic standards or personal integrity were quite different for these veterans, in comparison to their young counterparts. Whereas the young actors risked financial stability or career, the veterans risked harming their much-valued relationships with others. Neither was an easy decision to make, and each had to be resolved at some risk. Tina Packer, president and artistic director of Shakespeare and Company in Lenox, Massachusetts, commented:

> Obviously, I make a judgment call by call, and the few times I feel as if I've overstepped my ethical boundaries I've really paid for it. . . . I think everybody has their own inner compass, and I think that you violate it at your peril. . . . I think if you go over the line, you start destroying yourself. . . . I think you can destroy both your art form and I think you can destroy your relationships with other people. . . . I can

only say that I just do it the best I can, and the few times
that I fudged it too much it's been excruciating—in my
sense of my self and in the results.

The path traced in our study inevitably led back to the individual
actor. While supports could come from others as well as the individual, the pressures each actor faced—from family, peers, and self—
ultimately tested the actor's own resolve. When confronted with
difficult situations, student actors and young professionals gained
strength and energy from their passion for theater. Regardless of the
obstacles in their path, these young people still choose acting over all
other choices. Their identities as individuals are defined as actors. A
thirty-two-year-old Puerto Rican actor said, "My father's uncle . . . sent
me a letter trying to discourage me." His reply: "But this is who I am."

One of the hopeful findings of our study was that the young actors
were able to create their own opportunities and somehow transform
apparent obstacles into possibilities. When Jesse was criticized for his
"negative vibe" on the set, he appreciated this experience as a valuable
lesson. Next time, he would handle the situation differently. A young
Indian actor we interviewed said he considered bad auditions as
chances for growth, asking himself, "How do I fix that the next time?"
This openness and flexibility helped him to transform what some
might view as obstacles into professional opportunities. When he auditioned for the role of a Japanese immigrant in a musical, he asked
the casting directors, "Well, why don't you change him [the character]
to an Indian?" He designed his own costume, added an accent, and
got the job.

Despite the inventiveness and flexibility of the young actors with
whom we spoke, conditions in theater would not make things easy for
them. Market pressures inevitably affect the way in which actors ap-

proach the profession today. Film, TV, and the "Disneyfication" of Broadway threaten live theater. Most of the professionals we interviewed noted this challenge. "Theater, in so many ways, is something of a dinosaur because of movies and TV," actor John Lithgow told us. "If you imagine a hundred years ago, a hundred and fifty years ago, when theater was entertainment—theater, music, all of vaudeville, opera . . . it was so important, because that was entertainment, . . . back when you didn't have TV and movies. . . . Theater itself is a far cry from that now." The actors with whom we spoke were convinced of the value of theater for society, but the financial pressures on them personally, as well as on the entire domain, were patent. Though their resolve was strong, these young actors needed support and infrastructures in which to pursue the types of theater—both traditional and experimental—that are so crucial to the sustenance and renewal of the profession. Theater may or may not be in decline, but the young actors we interviewed faced unprecedented pressures and had to find ways to deal with them.

Like several of the geneticists and journalists with whom we spoke, a number of young actors admitted they are willing to compromise their value system in order to secure a desirable part and advance their careers. They expressed confidence that they would no longer make such compromises after achieving success; but they may have started down a slippery slope. It is impossible to predict which of these young actors will persevere and flourish in theater, and which of them will do so in a manner consistent with their own value system. But it is clear that they will be most likely to do so if they sustain a passion that enables them to override all challenges and costs.

5

What We've Learned

O UR STUDY GENERATED a huge amount of data, only a portion of which has been presented in this book.[1] We now need to step back and gain a sense of perspective. Rather than recapitulating—or attempting to make sense of—everything we have reported, we will instead note salient themes and striking contrasts. Chief among them is our discovery that younger workers are faced with conflicts for which they have little guidance: they must wrestle with these, reach a resolution, and live with the consequences. In struggling with these conflicts, they are loath to pass judgment on others; and they believe, in turn, that they ought to be given latitude to do what they feel is right. We are also in a position now to direct attention to the three overarching issues that we introduced at the start: comparisons across domains, comparisons across age cohorts, and the optimal path toward good work.

Three Trajectories and the Quandary of Moral Freedom

We have discerned three distinct pictures. Turning first to journalism, we've seen that young people who became editors of their school newspapers had a heady experience. They wielded a great deal of power over their staffs and had considerable autonomy in covering news and expressing editorial opinion. They received support from faculty advisors and enjoyed a captive audience in the student body. One important restraint, however, marred their freedom. As trustees of the principal vehicle of communication for the community, the young journalists were expected to support the spirit and cohesion of the school. Whether or not explicitly instructed to do so by their advisors or school heads, reporters and editors were supposed to put a positive spin on controversial events or, perhaps even better, ignore them altogether. Core values of the domain of journalism—complete and fair-minded coverage of important events—were subordinated to the overall well-being of the community that in most cases was footing the bill.

Following secondary school, most of the aspiring journalists in our study attended college, and many went on to some kind of further training in J-school. While not wholly dismissive of formal professional training, they rarely exalted their educational experience. From their perspective, the *real* apprenticeship occurred during summer internships and, far more, on their first "real" job. And while many would have welcomed mentoring, they were often disappointed in the meager amount of support they got from peers or older professionals.

The atmosphere surrounding the rookie journalists could not have contrasted more sharply with the one they had known when working on their high school newspaper. Having begun at the top, the older and more experienced young adults now found themselves squarely at the bottom of the totem pole. They learned that professional settings these days are chaotic; whatever supports may have existed in decades past, there is little formal mentoring today. Editors are demanding and unforgiving. The young journalists we interviewed had little say in what they covered. Indeed, their assignments included the most mundane tasks (covering the local public utility hearings) and the

most discomfiting (mandated face-to-face interviews with recently bereaved relatives).

These ambitious young reporters were often asked to do things they
would have preferred not to do. And not infrequently, they cut corners or even lied about what they had actually done (or failed to do).
From their perspective, this dishonesty was the price they had to pay
in order to advance in their profession or maintain their personal values. They were willing to pay the price because they aspired toward a
long-term goal: the opportunity to be the kind of journalist they had
wanted to be in the first place.

Turning to our second professional area, we found that the adolescent scientists we spoke with were serious and dedicated students who
from childhood had exhibited curiosity about the natural world, as
well as skill in working with small organisms and technical equipment. They had the opportunity, first, to carry out experiments in
their secondary-school classes, and then—often with the help of a faculty advisor—to find work in the laboratories of senior scientists. Initially, they volunteered as assistants and were assigned tedious tasks.
But from the outset they were exposed to the full operations of the
scientific world. They could observe the development and execution
of a research program, carry out experiments, and observe and even
participate in data analyses, oral presentations, and writeups of findings for publication.

In contrast to early careers in journalism, which are often impro-
vised, apprenticeships for aspiring scientists are essentially mandatory,
lengthy, and fraught with uncertainties. Attending and excelling in
college and graduate school are no longer sufficient. Nowadays, young
scientists often do several postdoctoral stints. In the course of ten or
more years of tertiary education, these students acquire a great deal of
knowledge, skill, and networking links. They often have the opportunity to work with several distinguished mentors. Yet only after a decade of training are they finally given the chance to set up their own

labs, devise their own research program, secure grants, hire assistants, and launch the careers for which they have been preparing.

The position of young scientists (particularly geneticists) today is very different from the one their mentors encountered some thirty or forty years ago. The older generation was working in a golden age, launching pioneering studies and opening up new scientific vistas. Today, competition is fiercer and opportunities in many areas have diminished. Young scientists can work for biotechnology companies and earn relatively large salaries, but they sacrifice autonomy in doing so. And so life with at least one foot in the university is still a preference for many.

Like our journalists, the young scientists with whom we spoke confronted ethical dilemmas. How quickly should they publish? What should they do when they found that a senior figure was behaving in a dubious manner, financially or scientifically? When, and to what extent, should they openly share their data and their discoveries? Should they let financial considerations affect their scientific decisions—for example, their choice of research topics? The time they had to invest in training placed enormous pressures on these young scientists to achieve a position of power and to nail it down permanently. And at least some were tempted to cut corners in order to achieve success.

In thinking of our third domain, we are struck by the fact that the young people we interviewed were attracted to theater so early in their lives. At first they may have been encouraged by their families. But with the exception of those families with a commitment to the arts, few families rejoiced when their offspring declared that youthful passion was modulating into a firm career aspiration. The very decision to pursue a career in theater often precipitated tension within a young person's family.

The young actors with whom we spoke were by far the most passionate of our participants. This is not to say that journalists and scientists did not like their chosen domains; it is merely to point out that the actors felt their career was the one that they *had* to choose. They found it difficult even to envision another calling. Perhaps, in contrast to the other young professionals, they were attracted to this domain for deeper and more personal reasons; perhaps the rewards they secured were more immediate; perhaps the difficulty of making a living compelled them to insist on the necessity of their choice. Cognitive dissonance can be a powerful motivator.

The transition from "school theater" to "real theater" may be smoother than the transitions we observed in journalism and science. Whether in high school or on the professional stage, plays are plays, roles are roles. Though encouraged, formal training is optional. And theatrical figures at all ages face similar dilemmas: Should they take any and all roles? What should they do if roles compromise their personal beliefs? To what extent should they cooperate with other members of a troupe, as opposed to promoting their own interpretations, their own agenda, their own stardom? Are their bodies for sale—and what of their souls? Should they countenance financial support from corporations whose philosophies are offensive to them? And on a personal level, what are the costs of maintaining love relations, of launching a family, in a profession that may at any moment require a professional to move to another city and to assume a role that annihilates free time for months on end?

As they confronted such dilemmas, our young actors resembled the journalists and scientists whom we interviewed. They were idealistic; they evinced a sense of integrity, and they voiced loyalty to their domain. Yet many came to the conclusion that if they wanted to have a life in theater, they would have to make compromises, at least for a while. They preferred that the decision be *their* decision, and not one made by a person in authority. The most difficult issue, as in other cases, was determining *where* to draw the line.

The participants in our study, then, were quite aware of ethical issues, of the myriad threats to good work. To satisfy their own ideals, they would have liked very much to perform in an ethically impeccable fashion. Yet, at the same time, they were ambitious for themselves and they were living in a time when competition was fierce, market forces were very powerful, and religious and communal strictures against misdemeanors were attenuated. Over and over, too often for comfort, we heard participants express their willingness to cross lines. Often this admission was closely followed by an assurance that when they themselves achieved prominence, they would behave in a different and morally laudatory manner.

Of course, such pressures are not restricted to the milieu of budding journalists, scientists, and actors. Wherever one looks in the early twenty-first century, one encounters fierce struggles to make sure that individuals—or their offspring—will "make it." Consider just one sphere—that of education—in November 2002. Those who were following the news learned about a thinly disguised million-dollar bribe intended to gain places for a pair of twins at an exclusive Manhattan preschool; an incident at a middle school where an ethics lesson turned into a theft and a beating; the decision of the University of California to force applicants for admission to document claims about personal hardships and extracurricular activities; a high-tech scheme to share questions on the Graduate Record Examination; and decisions by undergraduates to double-major, so as to improve their chances of getting into graduate school. How can youngsters growing up fail to infer that, in the march to success nowadays, anything goes?[2]

As we sought to understand the sensibility of our young subjects, we found resonance in the writings of two keen observers of the contemporary American scene. Political scientist Alan Wolfe has introduced the concept of moral freedom.[3] As described by Wolfe, "moral freedom" denotes a seemingly new attitude toward morality that has been adopted by Americans at the start of the new millennium. Americans have not abandoned morality altogether; they still believe that it is important to behave in a moral way. Yet they are extremely reluctant to judge the morality of others, and equally reluctant to allow others to legislate morality for them. Under the aegis of moral freedom, each person becomes the ultimate arbiter of what is moral, and each person is required to live up to that often idiosyncratic standard. As Wolfe puts it: "Now, for the first time in human history, significant numbers of individuals believe that people should play a role in defining their own morality. . . . The idea of moral freedom is not that people are created in the image of a higher authority. It is instead that any form of higher authority has to tailor its commandments to the needs of real people."[4]

On this analysis, individuals believe that they have the right to decide how to behave in specific situations. They reject the dictates of organized religion and the attempts of their superiors or of corporate shareholders to tell them what to do; and they may dissemble in order to gain immediate advantage. At the same time, they display confidence that any seemingly immoral acts are transient: as soon as they have the opportunity to behave in a way they consider appropriate, they will do so.

Quite independently of Wolfe's investigations, journalist David Brooks looked at college students at Princeton University—young people who are often considered "the best and the brightest."[5] The picture he sketches of these students and their contemporaries resembles the one presented by Alan Wolfe and reverberates as well with the results of our own study:

> When it comes to character and virtue, these young have been left on their own. Today's go-getter parents and today's educational institutions work frantically to cultivate neural synapses, to foster good study skills, to promote musical talents. We fly our children around the world so that they can experience different cultures. We spend huge amounts of

money on safety equipment and sports coaching. We sermonize about the evils of drunk driving. We expend enormous energy guiding and regulating their lives. But when it comes to character and virtue, the most mysterious area of all, suddenly the laissez-faire ethic rules. You're on your own, Jack and Jill: go figure out what is true and just for yourselves.[6]

Americans today generally assume that each person has to solve these questions alone (though few societies in history have made this assumption). Citizens of the United States assume that if adults try to offer moral instruction, it will just backfire, because children will reject their elders' sermonizing (though they don't seem to reject other aspects of guidance and instruction). Americans have come to believe that such questions have no correct answer that can be taught. Or maybe the simple truth is that American adults in a position of influence no longer try to talk about character and virtue because they simply wouldn't know what to say.

Initial Vignettes Revisited

At the beginning of this book, as a means of conveying the moral dilemmas confronted by professionals in the workplace, we introduced three young subjects. Though we described the dilemma faced by each, we deliberately did not indicate how it was resolved. We would now like to revisit each of our subjects, to reveal what they did and to discuss their chosen course of action in light of the themes of our study—including that of moral freedom.

Bill, the journalist, was distressed that he had to wrap up the story of the deceased small-town athlete in an hour, in order to give extensive coverage of people's reactions to the missing John F. Kennedy, Jr.

Trying to draw a positive lesson from this experience, he instituted new practices when he returned to his work at the *Harvard Crimson*. He compiled a binder full of stories that "really made a difference." He also encouraged student reporters to avoid sensationalizing articles. They should, he urged, steer clear of "trying to twist someone's words or get someone to say a phrase that will be useful in a story, in an angle that you've sort of contorted." Yet while trying to improve practices where he could, Bill became discouraged by current trends in the domain of journalism. "Perhaps when it's almost no longer possible to get at the truth because there's so many people working against you[r] finding it—that's when journalism will just become too frustrating. I hope that doesn't happen, but I think it's certainly possible." Bill was doing what he could on a local level, but was discouraged by broader trends in the field that he believed (quite possibly correctly) he could not affect.

David, the geneticist, was disturbed to learn that Peter, a colleague he had helped, was presenting David's work as his own. David's advisor wrote to Peter's advisor, and the latter distorted what had happened. On the account contrived by Peter's advisor, both students had been working on the same issue and David just happened to get there first. This incident tainted David's approach to his work: "I have learned that you have to be careful. . . . It's made me a little more cautious about telling people about results before I get a chance to disseminate them myself in an established form. I find that disturbing. I don't want to be that way. [My advisor] has been that way all along and I was sort of resistant to it. . . . Is that really necessary? I trust people." In the future, he said, he would have to suppress this cooperative and trusting inclination: "Sometimes reality hits you in the face. Behave differently—you don't like it, but you have to." Like Bill, he despaired of the possibility of altering a pervasive course of behavior that he deplores.

Martha was the actor who wanted to appear in a play about slaves in the United States—a work written by her friend Tom. To her distress, Martha learned that her fellow African Americans had all kinds of objections to the play, and to her participation in it, mainly because Tom was white. In the end, the production came off and Martha played her role. "I don't regret any of it," she told us. Though her first impulse was to join her community's protest, her friendship with Tom caused her to revisit the situation and consider the broader picture. "Okay, let me look at the value of the work. What's the whole picture here?" She concluded that the play had merit and that the protesters were pursuing personal agendas that seemed unrelated to the play. In the end, Martha felt that she was able to maintain a sense of integrity to the work, her community, her friend, and most importantly to herself as a professional theater artist. "I, to this day, feel I made a good choice." In this case, a young professional had to deal primarily with an internal conflict and was able to resolve the situation to her satisfaction.

We are encouraged by the fact that each of our three professionals recognized a genuine dilemma and sought to deal with it responsibly. In each instance a number of courses of action could have been taken, and a number of conclusions drawn. Indeed, in our study we encountered many subjects who behaved in ways that were less honorable than the courses chosen by Bill, David, and Martha: journalists who failed to act with "due diligence," scientists who rushed to publish a finding before it had been firmly established, actors who swallowed hard and performed under circumstances they found objectionable.

Still, across our study, it is fair to say that the young participants had an easier time identifying the course of action they personally favored than they did attempting to influence—let alone counter—the broad trends in their field: their moral freedom was essentially a personal one. Accordingly, they sought whenever possible to define a dilemma as a personal one, in which they lived up to their own values, rather than as one in which they had to go against the messages sent by figures of authority or by their peers. In more than a few cases, they decided to suspend their own values temporarily; they did so in the belief that laudable ends justified questionable means and with the confidence that one day they would be able to behave in a completely ethical manner. Rarely did they feel that they had strong support or guidance from others in their chosen profession. Only a few of them were likely to find the strength of character—either then or in the future—openly to dispute the norms and values with which they disagreed.

Comparing Young Journalists, Scientists, and Actors

It's time to turn to our overarching questions—the ones that could be answered only after our study had been carried out and all the data were in. We begin with a comparison across domains. The individuals attracted to each domain were quite different. The future actors were recognizable early on. They had begun to sing, dance, clown, act in early childhood; they enjoyed these activities, as did the people who observed them cavorting. And the transition to the acquisition of skill and mastery of the craft was relatively smooth. The passion for theater was lit in early life and burned brightly thereafter.

The journalists and scientists were more likely to have been conventionally good students, and, as such, to have a range of career choices available. Not surprisingly, the journalists were good writers and enjoyed writing; while perhaps shy, they enjoyed the camaraderie of others on the newspaper. They may well have been leaders of the school community, though they chose to spend their hours working on the paper rather than playing on the soccer field or burning the midnight oil in study. They often cited the importance of free speech and democracy as additional reasons for their engagement.

We've already noted the curiosity and skills of future scientists. Our sample of talented young scientists stood out in several other respects as well. Far more so than others in the sample, they were likely to come from immigrant families, to be upwardly mobile, and to report a strong religious background. They were more likely than other young participants to view their parents as hardworking role models and to look up to teachers as well. And to our considerable surprise, though the career they were contemplating was the most lucrative of the lot, they were by far the most likely to express concern about the amount of money they were likely to make. In contrast, the actors— whose financial potential was in most cases exceedingly modest— simply accepted penury as part of their career package.

These contrasting backgrounds suggest how interests can interact with needs. A different constellation of talents attracts one young person to covering stories or editing them, a second to enacting dramatic roles, a third to working with tiny organisms in a laboratory. At the same time, the social, cultural, economic, and religious backgrounds of families also exert an influence on the choice of career *and* on the personal and financial satisfactions to which young people aspire.

We asked our participants to describe themselves and, in the course of the interviews, we also formed opinions about their personal characteristics. The journalists were probably the most comfortable in the high school setting. They were diligent and dedicated workers, sometimes obsessively so. They enjoyed meetings, communicating with others, and putting out a regular product on deadline. Some indicated that they used writing as an outlet for emotional turmoil at home. By their own testimony, they were not a religious group.

The journalists in the workplace struck us in a less favorable light. Of the dozen or so groups of participants we interviewed, these were the least reliable. The case of Jayson Blair to which we alluded in the Preface was not an isolated one. The young journalists were least likely to show up for an interview on time, least likely to inform us they had to cancel, least likely to be apologetic for a mistake on their part. We do not know whether this trait—assuming it is not an artifact of our particular population—is due to the chaotic nature of their work, the attraction of a less reliable cohort to this career, the virtual disappearance of formal mentoring, or declining standards within the profession. As a contrast case, we can cite the behavior of a group of social entrepreneurs who participated in another part of our study; these participants, comparable in age and background to the young journalists, responded to our requests immediately and with admirable conscientiousness.

Lined up against the journalists, the high school scientists struck us as more traditional, even old-fashioned. They were more likely to come from families where they looked up to their parents, and where they valued religious beliefs and traditions. They were highly motivated to achieve within the society, and the success they aspired to included, notably, financial success. They emphasized the importance of integrity in their work, and they came off as perfectionists (though some did confess they had skirted the law as adolescent pranksters). The graduate students and young professionals were more aware of the dilemmas in their field and the costs that attend high integrity and perfectionism in a world that is competitive and often rewards those who cut corners.

The actors had the most fascinating personalities. They struck us as passionate, enthusiastic, lively, resilient, tenacious—almost promoting themselves in the course of the interviews. Whereas the journalists were sometimes irresponsible citizens and the scientists were matter-of-fact, the actors gave us all they had. Far more so than the other budding professionals, they were invested in their own personality and even in their physical existence. To use a current phrase, the actors were "all there" at every moment, and they wanted everyone to know and appreciate it. And perhaps more so than the others, they gave the impression of experiencing "flow" when they were engaged in their craft.

By their own report, the actors were marginal; this was especially true of the older performers. Often they felt estranged from the rest of society because of their cultural background, race, financial hardship, or sexual orientation. They gained sustenance both from the process of acting and from collaboration with others who were also marginal in demographic or other ways—for example, being nonathletic or having an exceptionally rich imaginative life. They worried about whether they would ever find a mate and whether they would ever achieve balance in their lives. The actors also reported a curious blend of sensitivity and emotional openness. On the one hand, more so than other participants, they described themselves as vulnerable and emotionally raw. Yet at the same time, they were able to mobilize themselves, to assume a range of emotions, to motivate and arouse others as well. They saw themselves as optimistic, tenacious, and disciplined; so long as they could handle their internal demons, they did not worry about external obstacles. Whereas the scientists did not deal with emotions in their work and the journalists did so through their writings, emotions were the stock-in-trade for the actors, young or old. And while they were not as conventionally religious as the high school scientists, many of the actors cited a spiritual dimension to their work—the theater as church, the stage as sanctuary.

When we consider the tensions reported by the young workers, definite similarities are evident across our three domains. While still in school, the young people with whom we spoke had a measurement of protection against these tensions. Mentors provided both cover and inspiration. Schools were likely to be supportive, so long as the students did not challenge the spirit of the community. And because career strivings were not so prominent at that point, it was possible for the individuals to maintain a cooperative atmosphere with their peers.

The high school students could afford to be more idealistic, and to honor the core values of the domain as they understand them. But when they were competing for prizes or prize positions—as happened in the Intel Science Talent Search or in the Spring Drama Festival at LaGuardia High School—their idealism was placed at risk.

Once professional training began in earnest, and, in particular, once the young people had entered the job market, their protective covering was punctured. There were daily pressures to kowtow to or manipulate authority, to crush competition, to cut corners in order to achieve professional success. Nearly all of our participants were aware of these pressures. How they construed and dealt with them forms the heart of our study.

Among the journalists at the high school level, the chief pressure was to place the school in a favorable light or at least to mute any criticism. Most of the young journalists accepted this stricture, though they varied in the extent to which they would defend it. Few of our participants attempted to circumvent it openly, and so we do not know how such rebellions would have been greeted. Yet there were definitely examples of school papers that dealt with controversial issues, and did so in a way that showed equal respect to the subjects of the story, the school, and the journalistic credo.

Once in the professional world, the journalists faced chronic pressures to sensationalize, to intrude on the privacy of others, to scoop their colleagues. Many felt that if they wanted to remain in the profession, they would have to make concessions to these pressures. Several explained to us that they could remain "honest at heart" while using "dishonest methods." Embodying the precepts of "moral freedom," they insisted that *they themselves*—not their editors, not the corporate managers—should be entrusted with that decision.

The scientists in high school generally accepted with good grace their "low man" status in laboratories. They were willing to work long hours and to pursue the scientific credo faithfully. When it came to competing for prestigious scholarships, however, they were sometimes tempted to misrepresent what they had actually done. Though it was possible to rationalize this behavior, these young workers had already begun a downward ethical slide that could prove difficult to stem or reverse.

For young workers, pressures steadily accelerate during graduate training and on the first job. In science, as in journalism, enormous value is placed on being first. And whereas a newspaper or evening broadcast has a new edition every day, scientific studies take months or even years to gel. The hierarchy in science is also well articulated; it is extremely risky for young scientists to challenge their mentors or other figures in authority, such as those who head funding agencies or edit journals. In the testimony we gathered from our participants, young scientists reported penalties for their honesty; pressures to cut corners in order to finish experiments quickly and publish the results; worries about the difficulty of sustaining a personal life when the most successful practitioners had virtually taken up permanent residence in their laboratories.

Since theater is so personal a domain, we were not surprised to hear actors speak again and again about the importance of being "true to oneself." In these cases, "oneself" could refer to the individual's racial or ethnic background (what roles should I take as an African American?), the individual's reaction to sexual pressures (should I flirt with the director in order to get a role?), or the individual's interpretation of a script (what should I do when I disagree totally with the director's take on this scene?). Though the actors spoke about the ways in which they could remain true to themselves, in practice they often found themselves in the same quandary as the journalists and the scientists-in-training. If they wanted to advance in theater, they might well have to make sacrifices: taking roles (or appearing in media) that they did not like, or acquiescing to an interpretation with which they had little sympathy.

RESPONSIBILITY REEXAMINED

A principal theme of our study concerned the individual's sense of responsibility to various competing entities. At a general level, our initial expectations were confirmed. By and large, the young participants in our study felt responsible principally to themselves and to those with whom they were in closest contact: their peers, their families, their immediate audience. High school participants—typically part of richly networked peer groups—were more likely to mention responsibility to others (and, in the case of the high school journalists, the "next generation" that they had to train). Beginning professionals— worried about their careers, in direct competition with peers—were more likely to cite responsibility to themselves.

As we turned our attention to the young professionals and to veterans, we found an increasing concern with responsibilities that extended beyond the local circle: the individual's workplace, the domain as a whole, the wider society. Thus, for example, the young actors reported a strong sense of responsibility to themselves or to their audiences, while veteran theater professionals talked about their responsibility to the domain or to the craft of acting. Likewise, though even the young participants were aware of the principal values of the domains, it was the veteran geneticists and journalists who—adopting the role of "domain trustees"—were more likely to speak of the responsibility to "science" and "a free press."

Even at this general level, exceptions emerged. Perhaps not surprisingly in this period of job fluidity, responsibility to the workplace (part of the "field," in our terms) was not mentioned prominently by our young participants. Yet the high school journalists did emphasize the responsibility they felt to their school. Among the young participant groups, only the scientists spoke at some length about their sense of responsibility to the domain—about what it means to be a good scientist. This finding suggests to us that the sense of a "calling" is strong in science, while it is attenuated at best in journalism and theater. Scientists especially, and journalists to some extent, were likely to mention a sense of responsibility to the larger society; and the high school scientists stood out by virtue of their own volunteer work in the community. In contrast, responsibility to society was mentioned by the actors chiefly in the context of bringing about social change. The actors instead emphasized their responsibilities to other people, particularly the audience. As noted above, the actors—especially the younger ones—also focused on responsibilities to themselves, rather than to people in authority; they saw *themselves* as the instrument for accomplishing all things. In contrast, both the scientists and the journalists noted their responsibilities to those in positions of authority—a responsibility that was often yoked to the power of the authority figure in the respective domains.

Not surprisingly, the younger scientists did not articulate a sense of responsibility to the same extent as their older counterparts. For example, in contrast to the senior geneticists, they hardly ever spoke about responsibilities to students or to the next generation of scientists. Both the young scientists and the young actors did talk about the greater power they expected to have in the future and their expectation that they would use this power—this "moral freedom," in Alan Wolfe's phrase—to serve worthwhile ends; few young journalists made this reference, perhaps because they did not identify strongly with the authority figures (editors, owners) for whom they worked. Indeed, like the veteran scientists, they often imputed responsibility to other stakeholders, such as corporate owners or the general public.

It is worth noting a few instances where young individuals assumed an unusual amount of responsibility. One high school senior was concerned about the status of high school journalism, both in the elite secondary school he attended and in less elite public schools. He thus devoted much of his senior year to setting up a consortium of ten independent school newspapers, with links to local public schools. Since he would not be able to benefit from this consortium himself, his institution-building stands out as a prescient and selfless act. Along similar lines, a college student set up a mentoring program for new students who were interested in journalism; he did not personally benefit from this action, and in fact passed up higher positions on the school paper in order to maintain this service to younger aspiring students. And an advanced graduate student in genetics (described in Chapter 3) noticed errors in a publicly available data set. He took the time to supply the correct information to a public official. Without giving the student any credit, the official simply posted the new data.

These examples remind us that even young workers can carry out impressive instances of good work. In doing so, they are presumably drawing on a strongly held moral code. Such young workers cannot count on being acknowledged for this work—but they can at least gain satisfaction from having done "the right thing." We were inspired by the words of a young graduate student in journalism:

Interviewer: To whom or what do you feel most responsible?

Journalist: Do I feel most responsible? A combination of the audience, myself, and whatever higher power guides me. And you can substitute that for conscience or something like that, but those three.

Interviewer: Could you flesh that out a little bit more for me?

Journalist: Sure. Is the product that I'm putting out on the air—is that of quality to the viewer? Am I misleading them? Am I offending them? So that's in terms of my responsibility to the viewer. My re-

sponsibility to myself—again, that mirror test:
Can I look at myself in the mirror and be proud
of who I am? Do I feel good about the decision
that I made morally, ethically? And then the
third: In the scheme of things, am I doing good
work for humanity? Am I contributing something good to this planet? Am I fulfilling whatever purpose I am supposed to, whatever this
earth plane is? And I don't necessarily pretend to
be able to answer that. But I think I have a
pretty good test for whether or not I'm on
the right track. Personally, professionally, and
spiritually.

WHAT DO YOUNG PROFESSIONALS VALUE?

We turn, finally, to our inventory of values. Given our research
agenda, we were pleased to find that the vast majority of our participants placed a high value on good work. As detailed in the Appendix
on Methods, these data are unambiguous. Across all participants, age
groups, and conditions, the values of "Honesty and Integrity," "Hard
Work and Commitment," and "Quality of Work," received very high
rankings. Considering the range of participants surveyed, and the fact
that they had thirty values to choose from, this degree of concordance
is remarkable and reassuring. Whether or not the young experts in a
particular domain actually lived up to the values of good work, at least
they believed them to be important and, so far as we can tell, admired
those who were good workers.

In the face of such a consensus, one naturally looks for exceptions.
Some were linked with the territory of the domain. The scientists
placed a high value on "Creativity and Pioneering" work; the actors
also honored these values, more so than the journalists did. For the

scientists, "Independence" and "Search for Knowledge" were also important; in contrast, but again not surprisingly, the actors placed a high premium on "Courage and Risk Taking." And in genetics, a profession where long apprenticeships are the rule, "Teaching and Mentoring" stood out as well. Across domains, adolescent participants placed a higher priority on "Self-Examination" and "Personal Growth and Learning." In contrast, beginning professionals were most likely to value "Rewarding and Supporting Relationships" and "Creating Balance in One's Life"—pressing issues for the young adult.

A few trends did surprise us. "Enjoyment of the Activity Itself / Intrinsic Motivation" was rated high by the young scientists and actors, but less so by the journalists; we surmise that current problems in the field of journalism may already be casting a pall on the quality of personal experiences. The pursuit of "Wealth and Material Well-Being" was cited particularly by nearly all of our male scientists in high school, who talked about the salaries in each profession, and about the weighing of intrinsic pleasure and freedom as opposed to securing material goods and creature comforts; it is hard to envision such statements being made by high school scientists half a century ago. We believe that the powerful market forces in U.S. society have pushed this value to the fore, and that the prospect of making significant amounts of money may be attracting a different sort of person to science these days. One has to ask whether the core values and mission of a domain can endure when individuals flock to it for its possible extrinsic rewards, rather than for its intrinsic appeal.[7]

One can look at the results of the value profile with satisfaction but also with concern. Clearly, most of the young practitioners shared the values of the domain, as posited by the successful veteran practitioners. That's the good news. But it's possible that pecuniary values may become increasingly seductive. This trend could bode ill for a profession—and particularly for the likelihood of good work in that profession.

Differences across Age Groups

Our second overarching question centers on the differences across age cohorts. When we compare the responses of our young participants with those of the mature professionals, we discern three instructively different contrasts. The contrast is most striking in the case of the geneticists. The mature geneticists, whose own careers coincided with the rise of the field, were an upbeat and satisfied group. By and large, they loved what they were doing; they were eager to get up in the morning; and the chief obstacles they confronted were their own limitations of energy and time.

The younger scientists were by no means bearish on the domain of genetics. But neither did they convey the sense of a current or imminent golden age. Indeed, like children growing up in very affluent households, they harbored doubts about the extent to which they could achieve as much as their parents. They were keenly aware of the competitiveness in the field, of the limited funds available for research, of the perils that might lurk in genetic experimentation. After observing the stresses of postdoctoral life, many voiced concerns about a career in academe. Also, given the economic downturn at the turn of the new century, they realized that biotechnology companies might not be as attractive in the twenty-first century as they had been in the late twentieth.

In our study of senior journalists, we encountered a far less rosy picture of the domain. Whether or not they referred explicitly to a golden age in the past, the majority of journalists were not sanguine about the prospects of their chosen domain. Overwhelmingly, they felt that journalists were not free to pursue their craft in ways that seemed right. Rather, they felt under relentless market pressures to cut costs, to headline the sensational, to "dumb down" the news. Consequential decisions about policy and coverage were increasingly being made by individuals without training in journalism—CEOs from the world of industry, "revolving door" politicians who were given key broadcast or print positions, or bean counters—few of whom cherished the rights and responsibilities of the Fourth Estate. A number of the veteran journalists were considering leaving the profession; only a lucky few found themselves at institutions—such as the *New York Times* or National Public Radio—that seemed able to withstand the most pernicious of the corporate influences.

The picture we obtained from the young journalists differed in accent rather than in quality. Even our youngest journalists were aware of these dystopic trends in journalism and decried them. Unlike our senior participants, they did place greater emphasis on the possibilities of a public or civic-minded journalism—one that deliberately attempts to realize a social agenda. Consider these quotations from our beginning journalists:

> I have a mission. . . . I have a responsibility to the whole community.

> One of the things that I think is important is, as that goal progresses on a daily basis, how can I affect people in better ways?

> I get meaning from the work . . . if I'm writing something that will, in some way, positively affect changes in something else.

> You get up in the morning and you really feel that you're doing something for the people.

> It's just that I enjoy the job and hope that some good will come out of it.

Still, the young journalists were pessimistic about their ability to effect desirable changes in their domain, probably because of external pressures to sensationalize stories. More than one-third of them reported that they were already considering leaving the profession; and more than half of them imputed the responsibility for bringing about changes in the domain to agencies beyond their control.

The young people in theater had chosen a profession that is older than science or journalism. More so than the young practitioners in other domains, they selected it for deeply personal reasons. Perhaps because of these factors, they were more accepting of the ups and downs of the profession; they believed in it ardently; and despite meager financial opportunities, few of them raised the possibility of abandoning the profession. They were much more willing to make compromises aimed at ensuring their continued work in theater; take up a sideline (such as tending bar or driving a taxi) that would allow them to pay the bills; or pursue a career close to theater (teaching acting, or performing in television commercials).

By and large, like their senior counterparts, the theater participants were not feeling the effects of strong and inexorable trends in their chosen domain. They recognized technological changes, which they saw mostly in positive terms, and pressures of the market, which they viewed less benignly. But in the long run, the essentials of theater would remain the same: individuals performing on a stage, "giving their all" so as to entertain, instruct, and inspire their audiences. Not surprisingly, our veteran actors talked more about their obligation to art, to theater, to the health of wider society. They were beginning to attain the status of trustees, a niche remote from that of the child performer who craves only the spotlight. All may have been worrying about their next role; few were losing sleep over whether theater would still exist a century or a millennium down the road.

Three distinct domains that encompass "memes," "genes," and "scenes." Three distinct age groups: teens just discovering the domain;

young professionals on their first job; seasoned veterans of the domain. Just about all of these individuals were striving to do good work, but their success was by no means assured. At the end of the day, and at the end of our study, just what can we say about the encouragement of good work?

6

Epilogue: Encouraging Good Work

INDIVIDUALS ARE CONSTANTLY FACED with decisions about which actions to take. Early in life, the
stakes are typically modest. But over time, as one rises in the professional ranks, decisions about how to act become more consequential
for oneself and for one's community. Also, an individual gradually falls
into patterns of expected behavior: one becomes able to predict
whether a given individual will hold to high standards no matter
what, cut corners whenever possible, or compromise only when pressures become unbearable. Such patterns become increasingly difficult
to change. Mobster Al Capone and humanitarian Albert Schweitzer,
by the time they died, had become quite predictable in their daily
actions.

Customary modes of action matter a great deal. Life in an institution or a society where most individuals strive to do good work is
qualitatively different from life in a milieu where bad or indifferent
work represents the norm. The norm of a milieu is rarely an accident
or a coincidence. It reflects the sum of actions taken over lengthy periods of time by many individuals, operating alone or in synchrony with
one another. If the *New Yorker* magazine is widely admired today or
the CBS news team was admired fifty years ago, it is because of actions
and practices that have evolved over many years and permeated the or-

ganization. If, on the other hand, Enron or Arthur Andersen have come to symbolize bad work in our time, it is not because of the isolated words of one CEO or the actions of a small cabal. Rather, an atmosphere condoning lax and unethical behavior was allowed to emerge and remain unchecked over a much longer period of time.

In our study we observed ethical dilemmas that arose during the first years of involvement in the domain. High school journalists had to decide whether to cover or ignore a controversial story on campus. High school scientists had to decide whether to report their laboratory procedures fully and accurately even when these could reduce the likelihood that the students would win a competition. High school actors bent on success had to decide whether to take on roles with which they were out of sympathy and, if so, how to interpret and perform those roles.

Over time, the stakes rose. Journalists on their first job had to decide whether to disrupt a bereaved family's privacy in order to get a story. Young scientists attempting to build up a vita had to decide whether to publish findings that were not solidly established. Actors in search of attractive roles had to decide whether to appear in a performance sponsored by an organization whose policies they deplored or whether to challenge a dictatorial director whose interpretations they found repugnant. In any particular case, it was difficult to anticipate just how a young person would proceed. Such dilemmas are the stuff of short stories, novels, plays, and films.

Six Factors: The Route to Good Work

We have identified six factors that determine whether an individual is likely to do good work. These factors do not follow a particular sequence; each emerges and remains important over significant periods of time. In terms of our conceptual framework, we can see the effects of continual interaction among the long-standing values of the profession (Domain), the nature of the particular people and institutions that currently make up the profession (Field), and the qualities of the individual worker (Person).

Long-Standing Belief and Value Systems

In most cases fundamental belief systems are transmitted by one's family. Often, in U.S. society, these belief systems emanate from an organized religion. But they may also derive from more personal spiritual traditions or from secular sources such as the Boy Scout oath and manual, works by Plato or Shakespeare, the Declaration of Independence, the Universal Declaration of Human Rights, or even professional texts like the Hippocratic Oath. When in a quandary, many individuals will consult examples from the Bible or other religious or spiritual texts. Once individuals begin to work, they may take their beliefs and values from the long-standing traditions of the domain. Ultimately, these belief and values systems are internalized: they become one's own personal standards.

Role Models, Mentors

Young people appreciate the opportunity to observe and learn from role models. In early life, these role models are most likely to be parents, other relatives, or teachers. As one leaves the home environment, role models can be drawn from a wider ambit. One goes to study or work with an individual who can help shape one's career. One also has the opportunity to learn from individuals with whom one does not have regular contact. Journalists admire broadcast or print writers; young scientists read of the accomplishments of major scientists; actors attend (or study recordings of) performances by masters of the craft. Some of our veterans also stressed the extent to which they learned negative lessons from individuals whom they did not admire; we call these negative role models "anti-mentors" or "tormentors." One's moral identity often represents an amalgam of practices and orientations gleaned from a number of these pivotal figures.

While our subjects often mentioned role models drawn from their chosen domains, and some reported fine mentors, we should note a broad trend that is disturbing. It has been widely reported that young Americans are far less likely than their predecessors to cite public figures whom they admire.[1] Either these young Americans do not cite heroes at all; or they draw their heroes from the ranks of entertainers and athletes, whose moral caliber may be low; or they restrict admiration to those with whom they are physically closest, such as family members and teachers. In an age where the clay feet of heroic figures have (often properly) been exposed, it is understandable why the young may spurn the heroic mode. Yet in the absence of examples that are in some sense larger than life, it may be difficult for young people to have high ethical aspirations.

PEERS

Especially in the United States, the influence of peers is substantial.[2] Involvement with peers who adhere to a high standard is likely to influence a young person to assume an admirable moral stance. Conversely, peers who have low or inconsistent standards can undercut a young person's ethical tendencies. One's relation to peers need not be passive, however. Almost everybody has some control over the selection of peers. Moreover, there is no need to follow the examples of peers blindly. One can argue with them, attempt to influence them, ignore their examples, or elect to leave the peer group altogether. Still, in the aggregate, the peer group almost always ends up exerting considerable influence over the ethical stance of a budding professional.

PIVOTAL EXPERIENCES

Many individuals single out experiences that have exerted great influence on their own personal trajectory. Consider what would have happened to three of our participants if an imbroglio had ended differently. For example, suppose that Karen had been able to work cooperatively with the younger interns at her newspaper. Or that Mark had been rewarded rather than marginalized for blowing the whistle on the offending scientist. Or that Meg had confronted the director for her stereotyped portrayal of Asian American women and that the director had conceded the error of her ways. It is too much to assume that these young people would have behaved differently forever after. But it is not too much to assume that a few experiences tilted in one way or another would be enough to set a young person on a more ethical or less ethical course—in other words, to constitute a "tipping point."[3]

INSTITUTIONAL MILIEU

Nearly all workers spend time in particular institutional milieus. When people are young, they spend their time primarily in school or in after-school clubs. Later on, young journalists are found at newspapers or broadcast outlets; scientists at university-based or independent laboratories; actors with a particular company or a succession of theater troupes. With the exception of young journalists' loyalty to their school newspapers and some biotech employees' loyalty to their companies, our participants rarely voiced a sense of responsibility to the workplace. Still, there is little reason to conclude that they were not affected by the norms of these milieus.

From one perspective, the institutional milieu may appear to be simply the sum of the models and behaviors of senior individuals (mentors or, less happily, anti-mentors) and of peers (others of roughly the same age or status). But this perspective is myopic. Institutions have histories. The behaviors and practices at any specific time reflect the philosophy and behaviors of individuals that may date back to the origins of the organization; and they are often bolstered by mission statements and founder legends, not to mention practices so ingrained that they are taken for granted. Over and above who happens to be at the *Washington Post*, the Cold Spring Harbor Laboratory, or the Guthrie Theater at a given historical moment, the legacy of earlier generations remains palpable—and it can inspire or stifle. And when well-entrenched norms seem to be violated—as apparently happened under the editorial tenure of Howell Raines at the *New York Times* during the early years of the twenty-first century—observers wonder whether there has been a temporary glitch or the abandonment of a long-term commitment.

Periodic Inoculations

For the recent entrant in a domain, each experience matters, and early experiences matter especially. To be sure, young people are not ethological specimens: there is no literal imprinting or critical period within which an ethical course must be triggered. Yet the kinds of "charged" experiences reported by our participants are the sort that can influence a person for years afterward.

Particularly at a time of rapid change and powerful market forces, early pivotal experiences—of even the most benign sorts—may not be enough to sustain an individual indefinitely. Mounting pressures to compromise, give in to temptation, and cut corners should not be underestimated. Veterans need powerful inner resources on which to draw if they are to retain their moral compass in turbulent times. Periodic booster shots may be critical. Opportunities to discuss concerns with like-minded peers, to join organizations that pursue an ethical mission, to participate in workshops or projects that confirm the root principles of a domain are invaluable: they may reverse a downward moral slide and bring the individual back toward a benign central tendency. Colleagues on the GoodWork Project have set up workshops on strategies for carrying out good journalism. Such "traveling curricula" have been well received, quite possibly because they give journalists the opportunity to strengthen a resolve that may have weakened over time.

No single one of these six factors is enough to determine whether an individual worker will lead a life of good work. They are better thought of as signs or symptoms. Yet it seems safe to assert the following. When belief systems, role models, peer behavior, pivotal early experiences, institutional milieu, and periodic booster shots all point in a positive direction, one is likely to encounter a good worker. When the signals are weak or decidedly mixed, or when they point collectively in a negative direction, one is likely to encounter a worker of indifferent or poor quality.

Supportive empirical data exist. In another sector of the GoodWork Project, we had the opportunity to work with young people who had been awarded Albert Schweitzer Fellowships and to compare them with a cohort of young scientists.[4] These exemplary individuals provided medical, educational, and other services to needy groups and communities in the United States and Africa. We found that the Schweitzer Fellows defined themselves in large part in terms of their responsibilities to others. They described service as an essential part of who they were and how they understood themselves. They identified important role models, most often parents, who had imparted to them at an early age the importance of compassion and serving those in need. These parents not only modeled hard work; they also modeled good work. The Schweitzer Fellows benefited from a strong supportive community of individuals to whom they could turn when they encountered obstacles in their work. Finally, the Fellows were engaged in a domain in which commitments to others were highly endorsed—in other words, the supporting milieu included both institutions that validated their practices and a career path that was admired.

We noted a lack of responsibility in the young scientists whom we studied. These individuals defined themselves in terms of their search for new discoveries, rather than in terms of responsibility to individuals, institutions, or moral percepts. Their work-related decisions were based largely on personal concerns and accomplishments (for example, winning national competitions), rather than on the societal ramifications of their work. Although they described their parents as hard workers, they (unlike the Schweitzer Fellows) rarely mentioned them as models of compassion or commitment to others. The young scientists conducted their work primarily in isolated settings; though they worked alongside other scientists, they hesitated to collaborate with others for fear they would be scooped. We posit that these young scientists did not express a strong sense of responsibility through their work because they lacked adequate personal, domain, and field supports. But we do not mean to suggest that young scientists will necessarily be irresponsible—indeed, most engage in voluntary community service. We assert only that they will have to stretch to locate the kind of personal and work supports that regularly bolster the members of the Schweitzer Fellowship.

Levers for Good Work: The View from Inside

When it comes to affecting the practices of specific workers, it is (perhaps fortunately) impossible to play God. One cannot summarily transplant belief systems, install role models, alter or replace the peer group of a young person. To be sure, it is possible to guide individuals to certain institutions rather than others (this is part of the job of mentors and, later, of headhunters), though there may not necessarily be a niche in the institution that would be appropriate. It may also be possible to encourage certain pivotal experiences, and to bolster certain tracks periodically. Still, one should not overestimate the extent to which people on the outside can manipulate an environment in order to control the quality of work and the attitudes of workers.

For these reasons, it is especially important to identify those steps that an individual worker can initiate on his or her own in order to increase the likelihood of good work. Our studies of veteran professionals have suggested three important steps that individual workers can carry out by themselves or in cooperation with others. Properly nuanced, they are within the sphere of young workers as well. These steps are not ordered; rather, they need to be taken regularly and repeatedly. Once again, they represent the productive interaction among domain, field, and personal factors. Conveniently, each step begins with the letter M.

MISSION

It is important to define the mission of the particular profession or calling in which one has enlisted. Of course, there will be traditional domain missions, and these can serve as a point of departure. But the most effective workers add a personal element to the mission as they understand it and wish to pursue it.

As we learned from our study of veterans, the journalist's mission typically stresses informing people—especially those who lack direct access—about what is happening in the world, so that they can participate intelligently and make appropriate decisions in their community. The scientist's mission is to carry out research of impeccable quality, to make it readily available to others, and to participate in key functions of the scientific process, such as peer review or the transmission of values and practices to the next generation. The actor's mission is to perfect his or her craft, to perform roles with integrity and passion, to preserve the great works of the past, to provide humanity in all its complexity with an image of itself, and to help to ensure a continuing dynamic theater.

Each of these missions entails service to the broader community. "Missionaries" will differ in the extent to which they instill a moral dimension in that mission. For example, some individuals in theater claim that social change is part of their domain mission, while others are wary of the risks of "agit-prop." Yet even those who eschew an explicit moral dimension see their domain as contributing in a general way to a better society—for example, viewing theater as creating a more vibrant populace or more engaged citizens.

Missions do not preclude personal advantage. In U.S. culture, it is proper for individuals to seek fame, fortune, influence. If, however, the *only* mission is monetary reward or personal self-aggrandizement, then one is no longer a professional—unless one wishes to join the oldest profession in the world.

How can one help young workers to clarify their mission and to pursue it effectively? If a mission statement already exists, it is useful to analyze it; to determine whether it is being carried out, and, if it is not, to consider how it might best be implemented; and, finally, to consider how it might be revised or updated. If no such statement exists, one could be written and critiqued. But the existence of "official" statements does not relieve individual workers from developing and reflecting on their own versions of the mission of a domain.

Regular reflection on mission by all the members of an organization is salutary. Such reflection is best carried out with respect to specific examples and dilemmas. (As this book goes to press, just such an exercise is under way at the *New York Times,* in the wake of the Jayson

Blair case. For more information, see the Preface to the book.) The kinds of conflicts described in these pages are provocative; discussion of such conflicts often clarifies the mission of a domain and indicates whether or not it is being appropriately pursued. Contact with "trustees"—respected elders who exemplified the mission during their career—is also valuable. Analysis of new trends in the profession, and how they might affect the traditional mission, is an important exercise. Fresh recruits need to consider how science can function freely and openly at a time when its perversion can be disastrous; or how journalism can be diligent and fair when sensational news is constantly being posted; or how live theater can continue when movies, television, and the Web are so much cheaper and more readily accessible.

MODELS

Most individuals are exposed as a matter of course to role models of a positive or negative sort, as well as to many who constitute an amalgam of attractive and unattractive features. But every individual also has the option of selecting his or her own role models: the people in a domain whom they would most like to emulate. Indeed, if a live role model is not available, one has the option of gaining inspiration from a paragon of the past.

The identification of a positive role model is an important step. Such models stipulate possibilities. They indicate what an admirable worker would be like. It matters that a young journalist can look up to James Reston or Katharine Graham; it matters that a young scientist can admire Marie Curie or Niels Bohr; it matters that Judi Dench or Paul Robeson are available as inspiring presences in theater. Young people need exposure to those rare individuals who have not been satisfied simply to accept the status quo, who have gone on to form their own institutions so that they could carry out a domain mission in a way that they thought appropriate. Every domain has its Ted Turner, who started an innovative cable news channel; or an Ellen Stewart, who successfully launched an experimental theater; or scientists like Paul Berg and Maxine Singer, who voluntarily instituted a moratorium on experiments involving recombinant DNA until such experiments could be undertaken safely. Again, it is perfectly proper for these role models to have attained worldly success: an ascetic or impoverished life is not a job requirement. But if these role models exhibit only self-aggrandizement, then they constitute a sad indictment of the possibilities of a profession.

Opportunities to interact with positive role models—and to observe the damaging effects of negative role models—are extremely valuable. One should reflect on the lessons that can be learned from such exemplary figures. No model is perfect; few models are so flawed that nothing can be learned from them. (Sometimes, unfortunately, role models come to be emulated for traits that are superficially attractive but ultimately unproductive or even pernicious.) Ideally, individuals become good workers by synthesizing the positive lessons that they can learn from a range of role models, while seeking to avoid the ensemble of negative lessons presented by less admirable others.

MIRROR TESTS

The quintessential ingredient of good work is the opportunity for regular enactment of a mirror test. When taking a mirror test, the worker looks at himself or herself in the mirror and poses two questions:

The *personal* mirror test: "Am I proud of the kind of worker that I am?"

The *universal* mirror test: "Would I want to live in a society where every member of my profession carried out work in the ways that it is currently executed?" Or, put differently, "Can each of my peers pass the personal mirror test?"

The mirror test presupposes honesty. People can always squint or obscure their vision so that they no longer see an accurate reflection. They can even purchase distorting mirrors. No doubt, some scoundrels confidently administer and pass the mirror tests. But the chances for self-delusion (or for deluding others) are minimized if one speaks publicly about one's own reflection (so to speak); determines whether it matches assessments by peers who are informed and candid; and continues to administer the mirror test regularly in as honest a way as possible. Hypocrites are individuals who claim to have passed the mirror test but whose hypocrisy stands at risk of being unmasked each day. Conducting the universal mirror test is more challenging to young workers; and those who subscribe to moral freedom may feel that it is not their job to take this test. But in our view, no worker can afford to ignore what his or her peers are doing. And if the work of peers is deficient, an aspiring good worker must ultimately attempt to exert influence on the rest of the field.

While the use of a literal mirror may seem contrived, the regular and frank use of a virtual or metaphoric mirror is essential to good practice. Only if one constantly reflects on one's actions and their implications is it possible to remain a good worker, or to correct course should one's actions fail to measure up to one's standards. And while some of this reflection takes place appropriately in private, workers are well advised to seek input from informed, sympathetic, but not uncritical peers and supervisors. Just as individuals need to stay abreast of the latest technical advances in a domain, so, too, they need to remain vigilant with respect to possible shifts in their moral identities.

Initially, of course, these three levers are not within the purview of the young worker. He or she is attracted to a domain long before understanding the mission in any detail. The role models available are an accident of place and circumstance. And there is not enough understanding of self, other, or options to make the mirror test meaningful.

Nonetheless, one can conceive of the development of a professional in terms of the maturation of the capacity to employ these three levers. Initially, veterans can help the novice in the domain. Parents can model good work in their own calling; professionals should monitor the impact of their own behaviors and attitudes on the young people with whom they work. Veterans can also articulate their goals and responsibilities and alert young professionals to the obstacles they may encounter and how best to deal with them. Gatekeepers from the field can periodically reformulate the mission of the domain and help other workers to honor that mission in times of turbulence.

More specific and imaginative interventions are conceivable. For example, in the domain of journalism, senior reporters can cover stories together with rookies—modeling, for instance, how one can deal sensitively with a grieving individual. Switching roles can be instructive. A frustrated actor can be given the opportunity to direct a scene—indeed, to direct the designated director in a particular role. Greater responsibility can be given to the young worker. For example, the director of a scientific laboratory may let a younger scientist write part of a grant proposal and give her authority to carry out the work, should the grant be funded. Gatekeepers can also alter the rules of the game in constructive ways: think of the implications, for example, if the Intel Science Talent Search were to give fellowships to students who carried out collaborative projects or if directors pledged to assign roles in nonstereotypical ways. We have even found that the opportunity to participate in our interviews helped numerous young workers to get a better sense of the enterprise in which they were becoming engaged, and to clarify dilemmas that they were or would soon be facing. Someday, perhaps explicit discussions of good work and bad work will be part of the routine formation of young professionals in diverse domains.

But aspiring professionals can also take the initiative in pursuing good work. They can begin to think about the broader mission of the activities in which they have become engaged; they can discriminate among role models and decide which they would like to emulate or to search for institutions where high-quality mentoring is the norm; and they can initiate mirror tests, striving to see themselves and others as representing variously attractive types of work. Moreover, the levers can interact synergistically: study of role models can help one discern the mission of a domain and one's own personal mission; disappointment with one's reflection on the personal mirror test can prompt one to search for more admirable role models or to explore further the current mission of the domain.

We can discern these levers in operation. The most impressive of the young workers hold themselves to high standards and can pass the personal mirror test regularly and comfortably. We are encouraged by the testimony of one high school scientist:

> I just hope that—I'm hoping that my generation and the people I come in contact with will be inspired to give more. Because you can try and reach, but you can't reach everybody. You can't convince everyone to do the things they're supposed to do. I can't force them to do something that I believe they're supposed to do. . . . But I feel if I make my small part, if I can make a small part, if I can play a small role, it will be okay. Because I've done my job.

One actor we interviewed was troubled by stereotypical roles and as a result created a one-woman show about her hero, the playwright Lorraine Hansberry. One postdoctoral scientist felt strongly that she should communicate her knowledge to the general public; and so, putting aside a manuscript that she was preparing for a scholarly journal, she wrote an article for the *Encyclopedia Britannica*. And one journalist wanted other young writers to have the opportunities he himself had had, and so he set up a local consortium to support middle school and high school newspapers in his community.

But too many of the young workers we interviewed were espousing a dubious brand of moral freedom—asserting that *they* were the ultimate judges of the ethics of their work. And too many of them were already squinting in front of the mirror—ignoring the implications of the corners that they cut, and perhaps deceiving themselves into thinking that such shoddy work represented merely a necessary detour on an otherwise moral path, or a stage on their course toward a position where they could act in a way that would earn widespread approval.

Messages

Society must become a place where good work is highly valued. Neither the United States nor other countries lack individuals of high intelligence, expertise, and creativity; but the entire world could use many more individuals who unite their considerable personal capacities with a commitment to act responsibly, ethically, morally. At a time when the world is inexorably interconnected and the potential for destruction has never been greater, a perennial concern with the implications and applications of work seems an imperative, not an option.

Traditionally, a link between virtue and technique was assumed. One can see this amalgam in the classical religious and philosophical traditions, ranging from the Platonic dialogues, to the Confucian analects, to the holy books of the major religions. It has been an important though dispiriting intellectual achievement to realize that there is no necessary link between technical skill and ethical behavior. One simply cannot assume that a proficient person will be a moral person, or assume that a concern with ethics necessarily translates into effective achievements. It is easier to be a good worker in one sense of "good" than to be a good worker in both senses of the word.

Having attained this understanding, however, one cannot simply accept the sundering. As Molière said, "We are responsible not only for what we do but for what we do not do." All citizens of a national and global society should take it upon themselves to encourage the development of young workers who are "good" in both senses. To some extent, this message will be conveyed to young people implicitly: through the opportunity to work with, observe, and emulate older individuals who are good workers, in settings that encourage and reward high-quality work. But it may well be necessary to encourage explicit tutelage as well. It may not be possible to develop degree programs in good work, but society certainly should be willing to talk about good work, to devise workshops that seek to promote its practice, to allot space in the media for presentations, and to point out with approbation those individuals who merit the appellation "good worker." Indeed, the mission of our own endeavor will approach fulfillment when young workers proudly declare, "I want to be a *good* worker," and trustees of the domain can respond, "You are well on your way."

Appendix on Methods

Participants

The participants in our study consisted of 104 high-achieving students and young professionals throughout the United States, including 32 journalists, 33 geneticists, and 39 actors. Because we sought individuals with the potential to become leaders in their fields, participants were selected not randomly but on the basis of their expertise. Therefore, they may well not represent young Americans in general. Rather, they represent high-achieving students and young professionals in journalism, genetics, and theater in the Northeast and can be presumed to generalize to a similar group of individuals.

Our participants were further divided into two subgroups within each domain. Because we were exploring the development of the young professional, we examined individuals at two levels of expertise: involvement at the high school level; involvement at the graduate or entering-professional level. Information on participants' levels and years of involvement in the domain confirmed the suggested trend (i.e., high school students had less experience in the domain than graduate students and entering professionals).

Our study of young professionals drew on research from another part of the GoodWork Project, the Core Study, which focused on veteran professionals in the same three domains (journalism, genetics, and theater). Below, we describe the sample of each domain, including these veteran professionals.

Journalists

The veteran journalists we interviewed included creators/leaders, gatekeepers, and midlevel practitioners. Creators/leaders were journalists who had received national or international recognition for their highly innovative work; gatekeepers were influential individuals whose primary role was to select or supervise creator/leaders; and midlevel practitioners were journalists who had achieved some distinction but had not been acknowledged as national or international leaders in their fields.

Reflecting the demography of the field, we interviewed more male veteran journalists (37) than female journalists (24). They were predominantly white (47), although 9 African Americans, 4 Latinos, and 1 Asian also participated. The veteran journalists worked in print, broadcast, Webcast, and documentary media; the majority worked in print or broadcast journalism, reflecting the current distribution in the profession.

Thirty-two young journalists also were interviewed for this study. Twelve were involved in journalism at the high school or college level; 20 were graduate students and beginning professionals. They consisted primarily of print journalists, though some broadcast journalists also participated. They were predominantly white (27), though the sample also included 2 Asians, 2 African Americans, and 1 Latino. Half of the 32 participants were male and half were female.

Geneticists

Most of the veteran geneticists we interviewed were creator-leaders (those who had made major discoveries and who headed significant laboratories at universities or research institutions). We also included a smaller group of midlevel practitioners (individuals who worked at smaller, less prestigious institutions, or held nonleadership roles in more prominent institutions) and several gatekeepers (individuals who directed leading national institutions but were no longer actively involved in research).

The sample included 34 men and 22 women. As was currently representative of the field, almost all of our participants were white; 3 were Asian.

The young professional scientists in our study consisted of 21 individuals: 9 male and 12 female. The majority identified themselves as white, and 3 as Asian American. Twelve high schools students also participated, but they proved to be a more diverse sample. Of the 6 males and 6 females we interviewed, 5 were first-generation Americans. The entire sample included 6 Caucasians, 1 Mexican American, 3 Asian Americans, 1 Syrian American, and 1 Greek American.

Actors

The veteran theater professionals were involved in the performance aspects of theater (artistic directors, actors, playwrights, producers, or executive directors).

As in the domains of journalism and genetics, the veteran participants represented the demography of the field. We interviewed an approximately equal number of men (20) and women (15). All were white, with the exception of 3 African Americans and 1 Asian.

The young actors included 18 males and 20 females. There were 25 Caucasian Americans, 1 Jamaican Canadian, 2 black Canadians, 2 African Americans, 3 Latinos (1 Puerto Rican, 1 Brazilian national, and 1 U.S. citizen of Cuban heritage), 1 Indian American, 3 Korean Americans (1 born in Korea), 1 Taiwanese American, and 1 Ukrainian American (born in Ukraine).

SELECTION

We used two methods to identify talented students at the initial stage of expertise. First, we recruited finalists of prestigious national and international competitions, such as the Columbia Scholastic Press Association, the Intel Science Talent Search competition, and regional drama festivals. Second, we recruited well-regarded students from leading regional schools in each of the domains, including Boston Latin School (Boston, Massachusetts), Phillips Academy (Exeter, New Hampshire), and Fiorello H. LaGuardia High School of Music and Art and Performing Arts (New York City).

To recruit individuals at the more advanced level of expertise, we used a nomination process. We asked expert informants to nominate exceptional students and young professionals who had demonstrated a marked proficiency in each of the respective domains. Journalism students were nominated by professors of journalism at leading universities in Boston and New York, by editors of respected print and broadcast news sources, and by other leaders in the field. The nominators for genetics students were genetics professors or department chairs at three universities whose genetics departments are rated highest by the National Research Council's Graduate Molecular and Cell Biology Program Rankings. The nominators for theater participants were artistic directors or training directors of eminent regional theaters in New England or teachers at leading theater training programs that were recommended by the regional theater directors. One of our nominators was the president of a well-regarded Boston casting agency.

Tools

As a means of conveying our procedures, we will describe the experiences of a typical participant in the study. We contacted John, a young professional journalist at the *Boston Globe,* and asked him to participate in our study on the development of young professionals. We informed him that there would be three tasks to complete: an interview, an ethics survey, and a values sort.

When John arrived at our office, we began with an interview that lasted about two hours. We used a general script to guide our questions, but we allowed enough flexibility for John to describe his unique experiences and express his concerns. Our conversation with him explored the ways he approached his work. It touched on his goals, practices, values, and supports, as well as on the obstacles he encountered in his work and the strategies he used to overcome them. At the start of the interview, John was asked whether he would allow us to identify him by his real name in a complete list of participants. If he said yes, he was asked whether he wanted to be quoted directly (he could reserve the right to decide after reviewing the transcript of his interview). All of our participants who were younger than eighteen were ensured full anonymity. In the end, for the purposes of this book, we decided to avoid using real names and to assign pseudonyms to all of the participants.

We next asked John to complete a survey that assessed his level of concern about important ethical issues in his domain—for example, being asked to report on the private affairs of a public person or reporting a story based on an anonymous tip. He indicated his level of concern about each issue by selecting one of three categories: great concern, some concern, or no concern.

Finally, John was asked to complete a values-sorting task so that we could identify the values to which he was most committed. We gave him a list of thirty attributes, written on cards, along with the following instructions: "We would like you to rank these attributes according to how important they are to you in your work as a journalist." John ranked each value on a scale of 1 through 5 (1 = Least Important; 2 = Less Important; 3 = Neutral; 4 = More Important; 5 = Most Important). He was asked to group the cards as follows: four cards in the Least Important category, six cards in the Less Important category, ten cards in the Neutral category, six cards in the More Important category, and four cards in the Most Important category. Next we asked him to select the four values that were most important to him as a person overall.

ANALYSIS

Interviews

The interviews were audiotaped and transcribed to ensure an accurate record of the participants' responses. The interviewers also wrote a detailed descriptive report in which they summarized the main points of the interview and recorded important information not captured on the tapes, such as comments made before or after the recording or made off the record. These reports were used during an exploratory phase to detect significant trends among the participants' responses. Researchers then developed a coding scheme to examine salient themes more systematically, and applied the coding scheme to each of the transcripts. We calculated agreement across coders using a statistic called Cohen's Kappa (see J. Cohen, "A Coefficient of Agreement for Nominal Scales," *Educational Psychological Measurement* [Thousand Oaks, Calif.: Sage Publications, 1960], pp. 37–46). According to this statistic, there was an impressive level of agreement among the coders, particularly for qualitative data ($K = .79$).

Interview data were further analyzed by counting the number of participants that adhered to a particular finding. This method added numerical support to the impressions gained from coded data and allowed us to make contrasts and comparisons within and across domains.

Ethics Survey

We used the ethics survey to identify participants' areas of greatest concern in their work. We computed average scores for each of the survey items, on a scale of 0–4 (0 indicating no concern and 4 indicating great concern), and then used these averages to make comparisons among domains and levels of expertise. For the domain of theater, we probed for ethical issues but did not pose specific dilemmas. Whenever comparisons were applicable, we compared the responses of our young participants to those given by veterans to whom we had posed the same dilemmas.

Values Sort

Finally, we administered the values-sorting task in order to ascertain the attributes most valued by our participants, both personally and professionally. To do this, we computed an average rank for each attribute across domains and across levels of professional development.

RESEARCH QUESTIONS

Our interview study was guided by the following questions, which we group loosely in accordance with the conceptual framework introduced in Chapter 1 (Domain, Field, and Person). We sought to answer the questions by looking at responses to our interviews and at other sources of data at our disposal. There were three other questions of import that we could not pose directly to participants but which we were in a position to answer on the basis of the data available in our overall study. We term these our "overarching questions":

Domain Questions

1. What do young workers see as the overriding goal or mission of this work? Do they think about issues of good work, and, if so, how do they conceptualize them?
2. What do young workers in each profession think about the world of work that they are on the verge of entering?

Field Questions

3. How do young workers view the current state of their profession? How do they think it will evolve in the future? Are they personally worried about the state of their chosen domain in the future?
4. What obstacles do they encounter as they attempt to carry out work? What strategies do they employ to deal with these obstacles, and what success do they achieve?

Person Questions Involving Others

5. Which individuals and institutions do young workers admire and why? Are there comparable persons and entities that they hold up as negative examples?

6. How do they conceptualize three major human spheres of their work: (a) their relation to older or authority figures; (b) their relation to peers, including ones that are cooperative or competitive; (c) their own sense of identity? (This last sphere involves self as well.)

Person Questions Involving Self

7. What are the principal ethical dilemmas that confront workers in their domain? How do they deal with hypothetical dilemmas that we present to them?

8. When encountering moral dilemmas, on what basis do they make their decisions? What do they see as their ends, what means will they countenance, and what happens when the ends clash with the means? Are they cognizant of these clashes, or, for whatever reason, do they appear insensitive to a tug between means and ends?

Overarching Questions

9. What are the common and differentiating features across domains? To what extent do young people in genetics, journalism, and theater resemble one another? In contrast, which factors differentiate individuals across these three domains? Finally, do the differences across domains found among young participants resemble those that emerged in our study of mature professionals?

10. What are the common and differentiating features across age groups? In particular, to what extent do the young practitioners and the young professionals resemble one

another? And how do these two groups compare to the mature practitioners in our umbrella study?

11. What factors contribute to good work among young practitioners? To what extent do these factors resemble those that we have observed among mature practitioners? And, finally, how can we encourage good work among newly minted professionals today?

Comparisons of Responsibility

Percentage of participants expressing a sense of
responsibility on various measures, by domain and professional stage

Domain	High school students	Young professionals
Journalism		
Responsibility to Self	33	75
Responsibility to Others (colleagues, peers, family)	100	80
Responsibility to Workplace/School	58	35
Responsibility to Domain	58	35
Responsibility to Society	67	100
Imputed Responsibility (assigned to other individuals)	0	55
Science		
Responsibility to Self	50	55
Responsibility to Others (colleagues, peers, family)	100	80
Responsibility to Workplace/School	8.3	15
Responsibility to Domain	33	60
Responsibility to Society	100	90
Imputed Responsibility (assigned to other individuals)	58	85
Theater		
Responsibility to Self	61	76
Responsibility to Others (colleagues, peers, family)	94	86
Responsibility to Workplace/School	22	0
Responsibility to Domain	17	71
Responsibility to Society	67	52
Imputed Responsibility (assigned to other individuals)	0	5

Note: Because the levels of responsibility are not mutually exclusive, these categories do not add up to 100 percent at either professional stage within a domain.

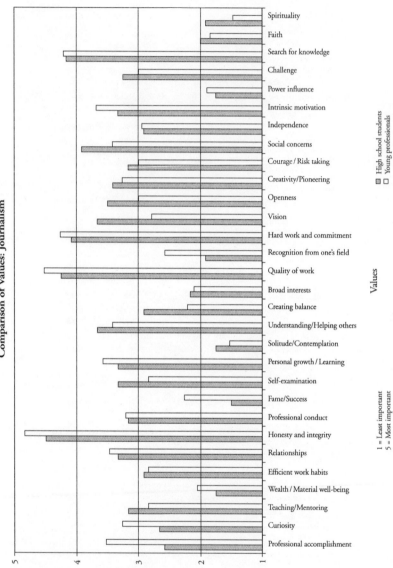

Comparison of Values: Journalism

Level of importance

Values

1 = Least important
5 = Most important

High school students
Young professionals

Spirituality
Faith
Search for knowledge
Challenge
Power influence
Intrinsic motivation
Independence
Social concerns
Courage / Risk taking
Creativity/Pioneering
Openness
Vision
Hard work and commitment
Recognition from one's field
Quality of work
Broad interests
Creating balance
Understanding/Helping others
Solitude/Contemplation
Personal growth / Learning
Self-examination
Fame/Success
Professional conduct
Honesty and integrity
Relationships
Efficient work habits
Wealth / Material well-being
Teaching/Mentoring
Curiosity
Professional accomplishment

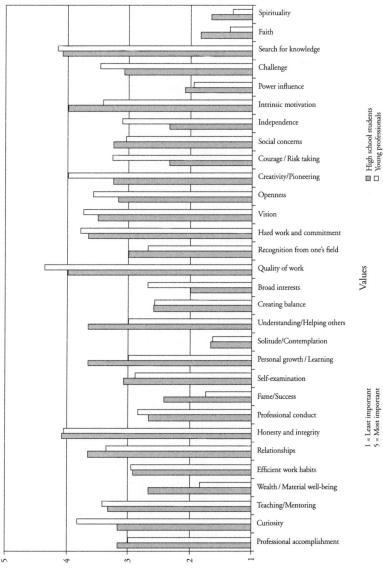

Comparison of Values: Science

Level of importance

Values

■ High school students
□ Young professionals

1 = Least important
5 = Most important

Spirituality
Faith
Search for knowledge
Challenge
Power influence
Intrinsic motivation
Independence
Social concerns
Courage / Risk taking
Creativity/Pioneering
Openness
Vision
Hard work and commitment
Recognition from one's field
Quality of work
Broad interests
Creating balance
Understanding/Helping others
Solitude/Contemplation
Personal growth / Learning
Self-examination
Fame/Success
Professional conduct
Honesty and integrity
Relationships
Efficient work habits
Wealth / Material well-being
Teaching/Mentoring
Curiosity
Professional accomplishment

Comparisons of Values: Theater

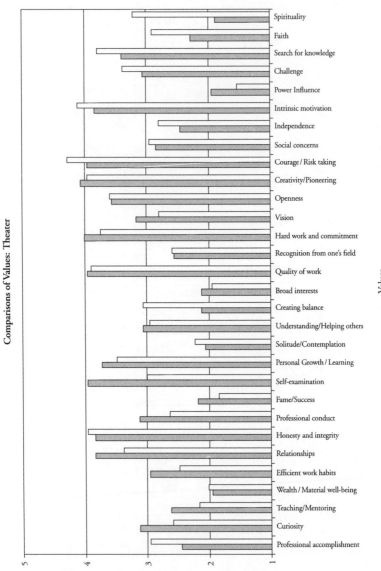

Level of importance

Values

■ High school students
□ Young professionals

1 = Least important
5 = Most important

Notes

1. Making the Good Worker

1 Quoted in J. M. Berry, "Fed Chief Says Economy Is on Recovery Path," *Washington Post,* 17 July 2002, p. A01.

2 For more on the GoodWork Project, see www.goodworkproject.org. This book will use the less technical phrase "good work." Conceived by the psychologists Mihaly Csikszentmihalyi, William Damon, and Howard Gardner, the project—which is ongoing—is a study of "good work in turbulent times." Eventually it will survey as many as twelve professions and will extend beyond the United States.

3 W. Chase and K. A. Ericsson, "Skill and Working Memory," in G. H. Bower, ed., *The Psychology of Learning and Motivation,* vol. 16 (New York: Academic Press, 1982), pp. 73–96; K. A. Ericsson, R. T. Krampe, and C. Tesch-Romer, "The Role of Deliberate Practice in the Acquisition of Expert Performance," *Psychological Review,* 100, no. 3 (1993): 363–406; H. A. Simon and W. G. Chase, "Skill in Chess," *American Scientist,* 61 (1973) 394–403; J. Sloboda, "The Acquisition of Musical Performance Expertise: Deconstructing the 'Talent' Account of Individual Differences in Musical Expressivity," in K. A. Ericsson, ed., *The Road to Excellence: The Acquisition of Expert Performance in the Arts and Sciences, Sports, and Games* (Hillsdale, N.J.: Erlbaum, 1996).

4 D. Feldman and L. Goldsmith, *Nature's Gambit: Child Prodigies and the Development of Human Potential* (New York: Basic Books, 1986); E. Winner, *Gifted Children: Myths and Realities* (New York: Basic Books, 1996).

5 H. Gardner, *Creating Minds* (New York: Basic Books, 1993).

6 B. Bloom, ed., *Developing Talent in Young Children* (New York: Ballantine Books, 1985); M. Csikszentmihalyi, K. Rathunde, and

S. Whalen, *Talented Teenagers: The Roots of Success and Failure* (New York: Cambridge University Press, 1993).

7 J. Piaget, *The Moral Judgment of the Child* (1932; reprint, Glencoe, Ill.: Free Press, 1948); L. Kohlberg, *Essays on Moral Development: The Psychology of Moral Development* (San Francisco: Harper and Row, 1984); W. Damon, *The Moral Child* (New York: Free Press, 1988); C. Gilligan, *In a Different Voice* (Cambridge, Mass.: Harvard University Press, 1982); E. Turiel, "The Development of Morality," in W. Damon, ed., *Handbook of Child Psychology,* vol. 3 (New York: Wiley, 1998), pp. 863–932.

8 A. Colby and W. Damon, *Some Do Care* (New York: Free Press, 1992); Kohlberg, *Essays on Moral Development: The Psychology of Moral Development;* S. M. Oliner and P. M. Oliner, *The Altruistic Personality* (Glencoe, Ill.: Free Press, 1988); R. A. Shweder, "Cultural Psychology: What Is It?" in J. W. Stigler, R. A. Shweder, and G. Herdt, eds., *Cultural Psychology* (New York: Cambridge University Press, 1990), pp. 1–46.

9 M. Csikszentmihalyi and B. Schneider, *Becoming Adult* (New York: Basic Books, 2000); H. G. Furth, *The World of Grown-ups: Children's Conceptions of Society* (New York: Greenwood Press, 1980).

10 M. Csikszentmihalyi and R. Larson, *Being Adolescent* (New York: Basic Books, 1984); Csikszentmihalyi, Rathunde, and Whalen, *Talented Teenagers: The Roots of Success and Failure;* Csikszentmihalyi and Schneider, *Becoming Adult;* L. Steinberg, S. Fegley, and S. Dornbusch, "Negative Impact of Part-Time Work on Adolescent Adjustment: Evidence from a Longitudinal Study," *Developmental Psychology,* 29 (1993): 171–180.

11 S. Cutshall, "Help Wanted," *Techniques: Connecting Education and Careers,* 76, no. 7 (2001): 30–32; D. J. Prediger, "Integrating Interests and Abilities for Career Exploration: General Considerations," in M. L. Savickas and A. R. Spokane, eds., *Vocational Interests: Meaning, Measurement, and Counseling Use* (Palo Alto: Davies-Black, 1999), pp. 295–326; D. L. Blustein and H. Flum, "A Self-Determination Perspective of Interests and Exploration in Career Development," in *Vocational Interests: Meaning, Measurement, and Counseling Use,* p. 345–368.

12 The SII and the CISS are frequently used protocols. See Consulting Psychologists Press, *Strong Interest Inventory* (Palo Alto: CPP, Inc.,

and Davies-Black, 1994); D. P. Campbell, S. A. Hynes, and D. L. Nilsen, *Manual for the Campbell Interests and Skill Survey* (Minneapolis: National Computer System, 1992). References supporting the validity of the SII and CISS include: D. P. Campbell and F. H. Borgen, "Holland's Theory and the Development of Interest Inventories," *Journal of Vocational Behavior,* 55 (1999): 86–101; G. D. Gottfredson, "John Holland's Vocational Typology and Personality Theory," *Journal of Vocational Behavior,* 55 (1999): 15–40; R. Hogan and R. Blake, "John Holland's Vocational Typology and Personality Theory," *Journal of Vocational Behavior,* 55 (1999): 41–56; J. L. Holland, *The Self-Directed Search* (Odessa, Fla.: Psychological Assessment Resources, 1994).

13 Csikszentmihalyi and Schneider, *Becoming Adult;* D. Offer, with the collaboration of Melvin Sabshin and the assistance of Judith L. Offer, *The Psychological World of the Teenager: The Study of Normal Adolescent Boys* (New York: Basic Books, 1969); A. Roe, *The Making of a Scientist* (New York: Dodd, Mead, 1953).

14 Gardner, *Creating Minds;* J. Bamberger, "Growing-up Prodigies: The Mid Life Crisis" in D. H. Feldman, ed., *Developmental Approaches to Giftedness* (San Francisco: Jossey-Bass, 1982), pp. 61–78.

15 A. Abbott, "Professional Ethics," *American Journal of Sociology,* 88, no. 5 (1983): 855–885; S. Brint, *In an Age of Experts* (Princeton, N.J.: Princeton University Press, 1994); O. G. Brockett, *The Theater: An Introduction,* 3rd ed. (New York: Holt, Rinehart and Winston, 1974); W. Goode, "Community within a Community: The Professions," *American Sociological Review,* 22 (1957): 194–200; R. Merton, "Institutional Altruism: The Case of the Professions," in A. Rosenblatt and T. F. Gieryn, eds., *Social Research and the Practicing Professions* (Cambridge, Mass.: Abt Books, 1982); R. Millerson, *The Qualifying Association: A Study of Professionalization* (London: Routledge and Kegan Paul, 1964); M. Weber, *From Max Weber: Essays in Sociology,* ed. Hans Gerth and C. W. Mills (New York: Oxford University Press, 1958); D. Wueste, ed., *Professional Ethics and Social Responsibility* (Lanham, Md.: Rowman and Littlefield, 1995).

16 Brint, *In an Age of Experts;* Brockett, *The Theater: An Introduction;* E. Freidson, *Professionalism Reborn: Theory, Prophecy, and Policy* (Cam-

bridge: Polity Press, 1994); W. Sullivan, *Work and Integrity* (New York: HarperCollins, 1995).

17 J. Fallows, *Breaking the News: How the Media Undermines American Democracy* (New York: Vintage Books, 1997); R. H. Frank, *The Winner-Take-All Society* (New York: Free Press, 1995); H. Gardner, M. Csikszentmihalyi, and W. Damon, *Good Work: When Excellence and Ethics Meet* (New York: Basic Books, 2001).

18 R. Chait, "Higher Education Goes to Market," unpublished remarks, Seminar on Higher Education, MIT, November 2, 2000.

19 L. Downie, Jr., and R. G. Kaiser, *The News about the News: American Journalism in Peril* (New York: Random House, 2002).

20 M. Csikszentmihalyi, *Creativity* (New York: HarperCollins, 1996); J. Rifkin, *The Biotech Century* (New York: Tarcher, 1998).

21 R. Dawkins, *The Selfish Gene* (Oxford: Oxford University Press, 1976).

22 H. Gardner, M. Csikszentmihalyi, W. Damon, and M. Michaelson, *The Empirical Basis of GoodWork: Methodological Considerations,* paper no. 3 (2002). Retrieved from Harvard Graduate School of Education, Project Zero, GoodWork Project website: www.goodworkproject.org.

23 See H. Gardner, M. Csikszentmihalyi, and W. Damon, *Good Work: When Excellence and Ethics Meet,* paperback ed. (New York: Basic Books, 2002), "Afterword."

24 For more on this framework, see Gardner, Csikszentmihalyi, and Damon, *Good Work.*

25 J. R. Harris, *The Nurture Assumption* (New York: Free Press, 1998); J. Youniss, *Parents and Peers in Social Development* (Chicago: University of Chicago Press, 1980); J. Youniss and J. Smollar, *Adolescent Relations with Mothers, Fathers, and Friends* (Chicago: University of Chicago Press, 1985).

2. From Cocoon to Chaos in Journalism

1 Thomas Jefferson to Edward Carrington, 1787. In *The Writings of Thomas Jefferson,* ed. Albert Ellery Bergh and Andrew A. Lipscomb (Washington, D.C.: Thomas Jefferson Memorial Association, 1903–1904), vol. 6, p. 57.

2 B. Kovach, and T. Rosenstiel, *The Elements of Journalism* (New York: Crown Publishers, 2001).

3 Ibid.

4 J. Iggers, *Good News, Bad News: Journalism Ethics and the Public Interest* (Boulder, Colo.: Westview Press, 1999).

5 R. M. Hutchins, *A Free and Responsible Press,* report by the Commission on Freedom of the Press, chaired by R. M. Hutchins (Chicago: University of Chicago Press, 1947).

6 S. Cloud, and L. Olson, *The Murrow Boys: Pioneers on the Front Lines of Broadcast Journalism* (Boston: Houghton Mifflin, 1996); G. Utley, *You Should Have Been Here Yesterday: A Life in Television News* (New York: Public Affairs, 2000).

7 N. Chomsky, *9-11* (New York: Seven Stories Press, 2001); B. Goldberg, *Bias* (Washington, D.C.: Regnery, 2002).

8 L. Downie, Jr., and R. G. Kaiser, *The News about the News: American Journalism in Peril* (New York: Random House, 2002); B. Kovach and T. Rosenstiel, *Warp Speed: America in the Age of Mixed Media* (New York: Century Foundation Press, 1999).

9 U.S. Department of Labor, Bureau of Labor Statistics, *2002–2003 Occupational Outlook Handbook: News Analysts, Reporters, and Correspondents,* retrieved November 26, 2002, from www.bls.gov/oco/ocos088.htm.

10 Ibid.

11 This vignette includes quotes from more than one source. The remaining eight vignettes in the book include only quotations used by the protagonist of that vignette.

12 P. Healy, "Tempers Stirred by Harvard Cartoon," *Boston Globe,* November 12, 2002, p. B1.

3. The Long Windup in Genetics

1 Editors' and Reporters' Guide to Biotechnology, Biotechnology industry statistics, retrieved September 24, 2001, from www.bio.org/er/statistics.asp.

2 National Research Council (U.S.), Committee on Dimensions, Causes, and Implications of Recent Trends in Careers of Life Scientists, "Execu-

tive Summary," in *Trends in the Early Careers of Life Scientists* (Washington, D.C.: National Academy Press, 1998).

3   S. S. Fisher, *Scientists Starred, 1903–1943, in "American Men of Science": A Study of the Collegiate and Doctoral Training, Birthplace, Distribution, Backgrounds, and Developmental Influences* (Baltimore: Johns Hopkins Press, 1947).

4   National Research Council (U.S.), Committee on Dimensions, Causes, and Implications of Recent Trends in Careers of Life Scientists, "Education and Research Training of Life-Science Ph.D.s," in *Trends in the Early Careers of Life Scientists* (Washington, D.C.: National Academy Press, 1998), p. 22.

5   Ibid., p. 25.

6   U.S. House of Representatives, Committee on Science, "Reshaping the Graduate Education of Scientists and Engineers: NAS's Committee on Science, Engineering and Public Policy Report," Hearing before the Subcommittee on Basic Research, 104th Congress, 1st Session (Washington, D.C.: Government Printing Office, 1995).

7   M. Nerad and J. Cerny, "Postdoctoral Patterns, Career Advancement, and Problems," *Science,* 285, no. 5433 (1999): 1533–1535.

8   A. Roe, *The Making of a Scientist* (New York: Dodd, Mead, 1953).

9   M. Csikszentmihalyi, *Flow: The Psychology of Optimal Experience* (New York: HarperCollins, 1990).

10 S. Hall, "The Triumph of the Brainiac," *New York Times Magazine,* June 4, 2000, pp. 52–57, 90–91, 100.

11 J. Youniss and M. Yates, *Community Service and Social Responsibility in Youth* (Chicago: University of Chicago Press, 1997).

4. The Price of Passion in Theater

1   U. Hagen and H. Frankel, *Respect for Acting* (New York: Macmillan, 1973).

2   U.S. Department of Labor, Bureau of Labor Statistics, *2002–2003 Occupational Outlook Handbooks: Actors, Directors, and Producers,* retrieved November 26, 2002, from www.bls.gov/oco/ocos093.htm.

3   A. de Tocqueville, *Democracy in America,* ed. J. P. Mayer (New York: Doubleday, 1969), p. 492.

4 *Talkin' Broadway,* retrieved August, 9, 2001, from
   www.talkinbroadway.com.

5 Information retrieved August 9, 2001, from the Actors Equity Association website, www.actorsequity.org.

6 Performance program for Bread Loaf Theater in Middlebury, Vermont,
   summer 2001.

7 O. G. Brockett, *The Theater: An Introduction,* 3rd ed. (New York: Holt,
   Rinehart and Winston, 1974).

8 Ibid.

9 A. Hornblow, *Training for the Stage* (Philadelphia: Lippincott, 1916),
   p. 14.

10 U. Hagen and H. Frankel, *Respect for Acting* (New York: Macmillan,
    1973), p. 13.

11 S. Callow, *Being an Actor* (New York: St. Martin's Press, 1984), p. 6.

12 Hagen and Frankel, *Respect for Acting,* p. 13.

13 Ibid., p. 19.

14 M. Chekhov, *To the Actor, on the Technique of Acting* (New York: Harper
    and Row, 1953).

15 Hagen and Frankel, *Respect for Acting,* p. 7.

16 U.S. Department of Labor, Bureau of Labor Statistics, *2002–2003 Occu-
    pational Outlook Handbook: Actors, Directors, and Producers.*

17 Ibid.

18 Ibid.

19 Ibid.

20 A. Cairns, *The Making of the Professional Actor: A History, an Analysis and
    a Prediction* (Chester Springs, Pa.: Peter Owen, 1996).

21 Ibid., pp. 59, 20.

22 Callow, *Being an Actor,* pp. 47–48.

5. What We've Learned

1 For more information about our study, including many technical papers,
   please see goodworkproject.org.

2 E. Gootman, "Students Are Charged in Plot to Cheat on Graduate
   Exams," *New York Times,* November 20, 2002, p. A25; D. Grady, "Sleep
   Is One Thing Missing in Busy Teenage Lives," *New York Times,* Novem-

ber 5, 2002, p. D5; S. Horsely, "California to Test College Applications for Truth," *Morning Edition*, National Public Radio, November 19, 2002; R. Mead, "Tales out of Preschool," *New Yorker,* December 2, 2002, pp. 41–42; J. Steinberg, "$29 Buys a School an Ethics Lesson," *New York Times,* November 20, 2002, p. A20.

3 A. Wolfe, *Moral Freedom: The Search for Virtue in a World of Choice* (New York: Norton, 2001).

4 Ibid., pp. 172–173.

5 D. Brooks, "The Organization Kid," *Atlantic Monthly,* 287, no. 4 (2001).

6 Ibid., pp. 40–54.

7 H. Gardner, M. Csikszentmihalyi, and W. Damon, *Good Work: When Excellence and Ethics Meet* (New York: Basic Books, 2001).

6. Epilogue: Encouraging Good Work

1 P. H. Gibbon and P. J. Gomes, *A Call to Heroism: Renewing America's Vision of Greatness* (Boston: Atlantic Monthly Press, 2002).

2 J. R. Harris, *The Nurture Assumption* (New York: Free Press, 1998).

3 M. Gladwell, *The Tipping Point: How Little Things Can Make a Big Difference* (London: Little, Brown, 2000).

4 D. Schutte, "The Development of Responsibility in Dedicated Young Practitioners: A Domain and Expertise Study" (Ed.D. diss., Harvard University, 2002).

Index